Dark Angels

Other books by John Simmons

We, Me, Them and It: The Power of Words in Business
   (Texere, 2000)

The Invisible Grail: In Search of the True Language of Brands
   (Texere, 2003)

The Economist Guide to Brands and Branding
   (co-edited with Rita Clifton; Profile Books/Bloomberg Press, 2003)

My Sister's a Barista: How They Made Starbucks a Home from Home
   (Cyan Books, 2004)

26 Letters: Illuminating the Alphabet
   (co-edited with Freda Sack and Tim Rich, Cyan Books, 2004)

Dark Angels

How writing releases creativity at work

John Simmons

CYAN

Copyright © 2004 John Simmons

First published in Great Britain in 2004 by
Cyan Books, an imprint of

Cyan Communications Limited
4.3 The Ziggurat
60–66 Saffron Hill
London EC1N 8QX

www.cyanbooks.com

The right of John Simmons to be identified as the author of this work has been
asserted by him in accordance with the Copyright, Designs and Patents Act 1988.

A CIP record for this book is available from the British Library

ISBN 1-904879-03-9

Printed and bound in Great Britain by TJ International, Padstow, Cornwall

Designed by R&D&Co www.r-d-co.com

For Totleigh Barton, March 2004, and the whole group –
with thanks.

what in me is dark
Illumine, what is low raise and support.
[Paradise Lost, *John Milton*]

Contents

Thank you

I have developed the ideas in this book over many years. In particular I have run workshops for people who must now number thousands, in the UK, Ireland, South Africa and the USA. Those workshops enable people to explore their own creativity through writing. First of all, therefore, I have to thank all my workshop participants. Each time I learn something new from you and recharge the batteries of my own enthusiasm for words. I am constantly reminded by your words of the innate creativity of human beings. And most of you have told me that you have gained confidence, pleasure and belief from your encounters with words in workshops.

I would not have had that opportunity, of course, without supportive clients. They really are too many to name and the listing would become like one of the more tedious books of the Old Testament. But in that Old Testament spirit I am particularly grateful to John Ainley at WH Smith in the early 1990s and now at Norwich Union. John's initial persuasion that I should run a workshop for his HR team 'begat' all the clients who followed after. Among them none has been more supportive or a more regular source of creative inspiration than Alastair Creamer at Unilever. If I don't mention all the other clients by name, it is not because of ingratitude.

Over the last year I have worked particularly with Martin Hennessey at The Writer; and with Neil Taylor, a former colleague at Interbrand now also at The Writer. That partnership gives me great hope that the ideas in this book will be taken up by many others. I'm enormously grateful to Tim Rich as a friend and reader, a provider of constructive comment and valuable insights. I have also learnt much from working closely with writers Stuart Delves and Jackie Wills.

My publishers Cyan Books bring an enthusiasm and commitment that are rare. Many thanks to Martin Liu, Pom

Somkabcharti and Linette Tye for championing this book. David Carroll has designed it with great skill, illuminating the words through images and typography. My thanks to Peter Arkle for reproducing the Guinness Travellers Journal illustrations.

I'm lucky to have a wonderful family, my son Matthew and my daughter Jessie who has also been a collaborator in this book through her photography. My love to them and especially to Linda who is an essential partner not just in my life but in my work in all its aspects.

John Simmons
August 2004

Chapter 1
Taking wing with the angels

This book is about writing. It is about encouraging writing at work to be more creative. Many people might instinctively feel that there is a contradiction in that aim: work surely is not a place where writing can be creative, except perhaps when you invite the advertising agency in to 'pitch'?

My argument is that the business environment has changed and continues to change. This means that companies, brands and organisations of all kinds need to be more creative in the way they operate. Only by encouraging greater creativity can businesses ensure that they keep generating fresh ideas. Reinvention has become the constant imperative, because standing still means they are soon left way behind. The standard tools of business management, as well as the teachings of the business schools, are designed to deal with what is already known. Like lawyers, managers are happiest working with precedents. Yet increasingly businesses have to deal with the unknown, the unprecedented. They need their people to be more creative to deal with that situation, for who knows what is going to happen next, how they can anticipate it or take advantage of it.

So businesses are becoming more and more conscious of the need to develop their creative abilities. Some do it through inviting artists into their companies so that employees can draw lessons from the creative process of, say, staging an opera, performing a ballet or making music as an orchestra. Those kinds of events are often worthwhile because they can be both enjoyable *and* relevant: they do help people to come together as teams. But at times we have to strain to find the real relevance.

Writing is different; writing is a business skill. Increasingly companies are seeing that creative writing has direct application to their writing for business. Many companies invite poets or novelists in as writers-in-residence. Indeed, I have been one myself. But sometimes that stereotypical character – 'the hard-nosed businessman' – still struggles to see the relevance of *creative* writing in a business. I am wary of being bruised or brutalised by a hard nose, but this book is an attempt to make creative writing in a business seem not only relevant but essential for reasons of business *and* personal development.

The plain fact is, writing is a skill that is available to all. Again, it is not only available but essential. I make one assumption about the readers of this book: you have to write as part of what you do to earn your living. That does not necessarily mean you are a 'writer' in a professional sense – although in my experience there are many people working in companies who are wonderful writers even if none of them will turn their heads in acknowledgement when I call out 'writer' across a crowded room. These people are good at articulating their thoughts in written words, get great satisfaction when they do it, but probably shy away from writing for much of the time. They might feel that there are more important avenues for their talents – 'I've got a company/brand/team to run'. Or they might lack confidence. Lack of confidence in writing seems to be a common result of what happens as education is followed by working life. Confidence gets chased away by those in authority, first at school then at work, and without confidence there is little creativity.

Of course, many people lack confidence for a reason: they lack many of the basic skills and thought processes. But it is my contention, based on experience of working with people to improve writing skills, that inside every mediocre writer at work there is a better one wanting to come out. They simply need encouragement, a little direction and a more positive working environment to release them from their verbal shackles. If we just take the example of business jargon, the sense of liberation can be almost tangible when people are given encouragement to rebel against it.

Rebel. There's an uncomfortable word in a business context. 'Rebel shareholders force chairman's resignation.' 'Staff rebel against working conditions.' 'Customer rebellion forces change of direction.' Can the act of rebellion ever be seen as a positive move by those in control of a business? It comes down to a simple view of the morality of behaviour at work. Most managers interpret adherence to the company's rules as a good thing. Questioning those rules is bad.

But morality is rarely as simple as good versus bad. Companies are discovering that to survive and thrive in the twenty-first century business world they need to give greater liberty to their own people to express their individuality at work. They are realising too that 'good' can mean an unchallenging and therefore stagnating attitude. And just as 'good' in that sense has little moral value attached to it, perhaps its opposite is not 'evil'? Perhaps the forces in opposition are not as straightforward as good and evil. Are we really talking about innocence and experience, mediocrity and creativity?

It's a commonplace observation that descriptions of evil are more fascinating than descriptions of good. So John Milton, writing *Paradise Lost*, made a heroic figure of the fallen angel Satan even though the objective of his work was to demonstrate the power of God's goodness. There is an aura about Milton's Satan that none of the 'good' characters achieve. And part of Milton's message, part of the attraction we feel as readers, is that Satan is an angel still: he has extraordinary powers of resourcefulness, invention and persuasion.

The question arises: would he have these powers, would he convey this attraction, without the opening up of his mind to other possibilities? Satan had dared and failed, he had been ambitious for himself, seeing greater opportunities for personal achievement than those circumscribed for him by God. God condemns him for his overweening pride and ambition. But really, as a management consultant might suggest, was he just 'thinking outside the box'?

Philip Pullman's *His Dark Materials* trilogy explores these issues too. The struggle there is between an exhausted ancient deity known as the Authority – represented by the repressive forces of the established Church – and the life-affirming, humanistic impulses of those in opposition. Again the angels are divided, and our sympathies are engaged by the flawed dark angels. The struggle is against the good angels of the Church that seeks to keep people in a state of 'innocence' deprived of 'experience'. Innocence is a state that deprives us of the possibility of making a choice between good and evil, or actually between thinking and not thinking, between feeling and not feeling. Having the choice is what matters: without it we are creatures without a real moral dimension. We remain creatures without experience, without the ability to think, question and create.

We live in a world where the dark angels have lived. Perhaps we have become like dark angels ourselves. As a result, we have the ability to express individual personalities. Dark angels are symbols of that ability; they are not symbols of evil. If we fail to respond to their challenge, we retreat into a working life of meek, unquestioning acceptance of our innocent role. We follow the unwritten rules of the organisation's custom and practice, and we leave our emotional engagement for other times and other places. We fall into the working life of accepting that we have a limited desire or ambition to influence things, to imagine other possibilities, to fulfil ourselves, to achieve intellectual goals.

Too often, at work, we behave as if the Authority rules. We need to embrace possibilities offered by the dark angels, to see that our destiny can be brighter if we explore, develop and fulfil the deeper, darker reaches of our creativity.

In this book I aim to help people who need to write at work (that means most of you) to understand better how they can explore and use their own creativity with language. This book is for anyone who wants to become a better writer at work. I have tried, but failed, to imagine who might resist that objective. If you want to be better at your job – for reasons of personal satisfaction, financial gain or any other motivation – writing will help you. It will help you to communicate more clearly, to make arguments more effectively. But, if we go further, more expressive writing will help you to establish greater personal authority and be respected as someone who should be heeded. And then, if we go further again, more creative writing will help you tell stories better, engage with people, make emotional connections that mean other people really enjoy what you are communicating.

If this means you become a dark angel, don't worry. It's just a matter of spreading your wings.

So come fly with me.

Who needs to write at work? I could fill the next two hundred pages with job titles. Accident insurers, accommodation salespeople, accountants through to zeitgeist consultants, zip manufacturers and zookeepers. It's hard to think of a job that does not require the use of words, in spoken if not written form. Some jobs are done without committing a single word to paper or computer memory. Perhaps these jobs too would be done better if the written word played a greater role in them.

The fact is we all need to think if we are to be effective. And 'How do you think if you don't use words?' That plaintive question was spoken from the tiny screen on the back of the seat in front of me, as I crossed the Atlantic watching Judi Dench play Iris Murdoch. Iris's fear, of course, was that Alzheimer's would rob her of her ability to use words, to think. It's a fear we can all share, so let's not succumb to a kind of voluntary Alzheimer's at work. Exercise your brain by exercising your writing ability. See what fresh thoughts emerge.

The reality is that if we write at work on behalf of a company, organisation or brand we are being asked to carry out a creative writing exercise. The task might be to write the chairman's statement or speech, to produce the words that go on packaging, to write a proposal to win new business or a report to persuade colleagues to do something different. In any of these cases you will be writing in a persona that incorporates some of your own personality as well as that of your organisation. Creativity is never 'pure', it does not come from some spring of inspiration that has no connection to us; imagination is always rooted in our own experience and memory. All novelists put something of themselves into every character they write. Dickens put a lot of himself into David Copperfield but also much of himself into Fagin. So, if we are to become better writers at work, we need to develop creative writing skills – and stop feeling embarrassed or guilty about it. Indeed we need to realise that this is the way to become better at our jobs, because the effective use of words is an essential skill at work. To be effective we need to be creative. Companies need to produce more writing that is creative.

Most advice on improving business writing skills focuses on the virtues of 'plain English'. My quarrel with that is that it seems a hopelessly limited ambition to want to write plain and nothing but plain. How many people get tempted into a beauty treatment that promises 'we'll make you look really plain'? 'Plain' might mean simple, straightforward and clear – virtues for some kinds of writing – but few of us choose a plainly written novel to read.

Novels are very different from annual reports. Of course they are. The differences became greater when hard noses scented the possibility, as the last century advanced, of banishing imagination from their world of cold reason. Yet we still choose novels to read because we seek entertainment, insight, connection into another world outside ourselves, understanding of some deeper truths about ourselves and others. What if we were to seek some of the same things from business writing: entertainment, insight, connection, understanding? Do we simply have to look for facts and information from business writing, or is it possible, even desirable, to ask for more? My contention is that we should at least try.

More creative business writing benefits both the writers and the readers. Writers are liberated to explore a wider range of emotions and thoughts inside themselves, and put more of themselves into their work. This has to be preferred to the constrictions of putting simply the most practical and rational part of their personalities into their writing – after all, how many of us are simply practical and rational? We are human beings. Part of our human nature is to be practical and rational, in effect to follow a plan and obey orders; but there is much more to being human. We are emotional, subjective beings, we are swayed by feelings not just by facts. The most persuasive communication connects to our emotions as well as to our reason. Exploring individual creativity within our personalities is liberating for those given the encouragement to do so. It increases enthusiasm for work, improves job satisfaction – and makes people much better at an essential aspect of what we all have to do: persuade others.

Better creative writing benefits the readers too. Readers can choose between a piece of writing that is alive with personality or inert with plain information. The live writing engages their interest and emotions. They absorb the information better; it brightens their day instead of just being part of life's dullest wallpaper. Reading more imaginative writing stimulates the reader's own imagination.

That also arouses a feeling of affection and gratitude. The benefits for the individual writer and reader are real, but the company, organisation or brand becomes the channel through which these positive feelings flow. People feel greater loyalty to the corporate entity as a result, and the business benefits are tangible, not just linked to softer issues of encouraging personal development among employees.

Businesses need to behave less like the Authority. They need to trust their people more. If not they'll live in a state of perpetual anxiety about getting people to conform to rules and about developing in a circumscribed way. Brands that are strong have rules but are less obsessed about them; they rely more on creating an intuitive understanding of what they are about. And they are generally about having a more interesting personality that further encourages individual expression. There is a misconception that identity and branding are primarily about uniformity: they need to be about uniformity only when the nature of the organisation demands it. Perhaps the organisation with the most uniform identity in the world is North Korea. How many brands want to emulate North Korea?

In a debate at the National Theatre between Philip Pullman and the Archbishop of Canterbury, Rowan Williams, the expectation of many was that the Archbishop would reject and condemn Pullman's *His Dark Materials*. His acceptance, indeed enthusiasm for the author and his works, surprised those in the audience with fundamentalist leanings.

If the Authority is not God, why has the historic Church so often behaved as if it did exist to protect a mortal and finite God? What would a church life look like that actually expressed the reality of a divine freedom enabling human freedom?
[Rowan Williams in the Guardian]

Many of you reading this book will be the archbishops, clergy and congregation of the working world. You have it in your power to express the reality of an organisational freedom that enables human freedom. Writing is the most accessible resource you have to enable that freedom. You are a dark angel; we all are. You can soar out of the place where you have been confined. Just use your wings.

Chapter 2
The first short steps

So you want to become a better writer at work? You have put your hand up.

But let me put my hand up first. We might as well get the unpalatable news out of the way quickly. You don't ever reach a point where you can't become a better writer. It's a matter of constant practice, you always need to work at it to get better. You become that painter of the Forth Bridge: by the time you reach one side you have to go back and start again.

What I believe is possible – and this is the more optimistic slant that I always look for – is that we can each reach a point where this task we've set ('becoming a better writer') is not an irritating chore, not an impossibly daunting task. Because what happens is that we develop such a love for words and writing that we approach the task with a light not a heavy heart, with enthusiasm not dread. If you're not yet at that point, I hope during the course of this book to move you a little bit closer to it. And perhaps the best way into that state of mind is by concentrating first on 'writing short'.

By 'writing short' I refer to those communications where we have to say as much as possible in as few words as possible. Emails are one example. The words that go on packaging are another, or the executive summary of a proposal to the board. Of course, they are all different: the only thing that unites them is a shared need to be concise so that we don't lose the attention of the reader. But I don't see 'writing for business' as living in a completely different ghetto from other kinds of writing. I will, therefore, be using examples from poetry, another form of writing which is about trying to say as much as possible in as few words as possible.

Here are three definitions of poetry:

Poetry is the best words in the best order
[Samuel Taylor Coleridge]

Poetry is the art of using words charged with their utmost meaning
[Dana Gioia]

Poetry is that which arrives at the intellect by way of the heart
   [R. S. Thomas]

It sounds tough but I'd like all our writing to aspire to those definitions. Yes, even – perhaps especially – that last one. Heart as well as intellect.

Even short writing needs a structure. I wondered about the structure of this chapter with the radio playing in the background. The programme was *Desert Island Discs*. I'm unlikely ever to be invited onto the programme to select my favourite music but that need not stop me – or you – from coming up with a list. This became my structural starting point for this chapter. So I have to choose eight records that mean something to me and that can be used to illustrate points about writing short in particular. Because my choices will be mainly songs, they themselves represent examples of short writing. Storytelling is another fundamental part of writing, so I will also tell you the story that lies behind my choice of song in each case.

My first record is *Hejira* by Joni Mitchell. I have a number of reasons for choosing this. First, I think it's a wonderful song. But it reminds me of two particular times in my life. First, listening to this in the mid-seventies when my children were being born and I was particularly aware of passing from one stage of life to another. And, then, more recently, when we had a poetry event at Lever Fabergé on National Poetry Day in 2002 and Alastair Creamer brought along, as a poem to read, *Hejira* by Joni Mitchell.

I know no-one's going to show me everything
We all come and go unknown
Each so deep and superficial
Between the forceps and the stone

That tiny extract conveys a lot in a few words. First 'Each so deep and superficial'. Take away one of the adjectives and it becomes a trite statement. Put the two together, because they are opposite in meaning, you are asked to think more clearly about the meaning of each word. So that line provokes a thought about how we can give fresh meanings to words that we perhaps take for granted. Our words should not be inert, they should be charged with meaning. We have to think about each one, so that our reader will also be encouraged to think about what we're trying to say.

The second thing to pick up on is the phrase 'Between the forceps and the stone'. It's a variant on 'from cradle to grave', which we've become a little too accustomed to. Metaphors that start life vivid and fresh can turn into clichés through repeated use. We have to think a little about Joni Mitchell's metaphor, but in thinking we have images in our heads of the forceps that help bring a baby into life and the stone that marks the end of it. It's said through a few short, not necessarily plain, words that have been carefully and imaginatively chosen.

'Hejira' is the word used to describe Mohammed's flight from Mecca. It has associations of flight and pilgrimage and travelling. If we are in flight we are travelling, but with a definite purpose. The purpose gives an edge of anxiety to our travelling. Too often at work we are simply coasting, passing through, rather than travelling with a purpose. At our most undemanding we become tourists, seeking out the equivalent of the deck-chair under a sun-shade. But a year-long beach holiday becomes boring after a time; it restricts our ability to seek and enjoy novelty. Often, if our jobs are not challenging enough in themselves, we need to seek novelty – not necessarily by changing jobs but by introducing our own challenges into a job. Writing is a way to introduce that element of challenge.

It's about the difference between being a traveller and a tourist. We all have that choice, not only when we go on holiday, but each day that we work. Choose to make writing a vital element of your work. We each have the choice to make. We can go and sit on the beach, but actually we could be more or less anywhere as long as there is sunshine. Or we can be more curious about where we are, the things that are around us, the people we meet.

So, accompanying my first record is my first principle of writing:

Be curious. Be a traveller not a tourist. Be open to possibilities.

Try this as an experiment. Take any piece of your own writing and apply this principle to it. See how you might write it differently to convey a greater sense of your own curiosity. What happens, for example, if you rewrite a paragraph of dry, factual statements as a series of questions? Clearly the tone is going to be less definite; perhaps it will seem too weak and uncertain. Or perhaps the questions will introduce an interesting sense of inquisitiveness. That might then lead your thinking in a completely different direction.

The second *Desert Island* record is by an Icelandic band called Sigur Ros. I first came across them about a year ago when my son gave me one of their records as a present. He just said 'you'll like this' and he was right. It's ethereal music, sounding to me as if it could only be from the northern parts of the northern hemisphere. It's largely instrumental but there are individuals and choirs singing words which I assumed were Icelandic. I was later told that many of the words are in a language invented by the band, which they call Hopelandish.

Svefn-g-englar
Staralfur
Flugufrelsarinn
Ny batteri
Hjartad hammast
Vidrar vel til lottarasa
Olsen olsen
Agaetis byrjun
Avalon

We haven't a clue what it means. Except you sense something, you read something into it. And at the end, there is a word that's more familiar – Avalon. Avalon, a name from mythology. And even though we couldn't pin down the actual meaning of any of those words, there is a kind of storytelling going on. This is reinforced when you listen to the music too. It sounds to me like the soundtrack to accompany Philip Pullman's book *Northern Lights*.

When we're writing we need to be conscious that our readers will be using their senses; in particular they will be seeing and hearing. Words are not absorbed just by our brains. We can put images with words and each will reinforce the other. And, particularly when we're writing material that is going to be designed – for example, on a pack – we need to be aware of how our words will be seen in a visual context.

But our words will be heard too. It's probably rare that someone in a supermarket will declaim the words on packaging. But we need to be aware of two things that relate to listening. First the readers will, without really being aware of it, be hearing the words in their heads. From the words they will deduce a particular tone of voice, they will draw conclusions about the writer's personality. Here's something I worked on for Birds Eye. It's the Birds Eye Promise as seen on different packs.

Birds Eye peas are frozen for a good reason – it's the most natural way to preserve them. We do it within 2½ hours of picking so that we can guarantee you locked-in vitamin goodness. From field to fork our farmers are committed to quality, caring for their pea crop and the long-term health of the environment. What's more – we're working to make our peas, and farming practices, even better in the future.

Fresh from the sea and frozen to lock in all the goodness, we select only the finest quality of fish. Everything in our range is frozen for a good reason – it's the most natural way to preserve food. We don't add artificial colours or flavours, we simply bring you tasty, wholesome food. Of course, we won't stop there, we'll keep working towards responsible fishing practices and to make our food even better for you.

Birds Eye Waffles are frozen for a very good reason – it's nature's way to preserve food. We don't add any artificial colours, flavours or preservatives. What's more our waffles are only cooked in sunflower oil, which is low in saturated fat, and are checked for quality by someone called Brian. He counts the holes and ensures they're all the right shape. What a great guy.

The tone of voice varies from product to product, Promise to Promise, and there's no problem with that because the product personality is different in each case. But we all need to be aware of this process happening – of people listening to our words, drawing conclusions, making assumptions. To like us or not? So the words matter, and we need to craft them.

In the case of words that appear on food packaging, space is always going to be limited. So is your reader's attention span. Imagine a mother with one child sat in the supermarket trolley and another tugging at her legs. You don't really have a second or word to waste. But you can provide short, sharp information to read in-store and more relaxed copy – like the Promise – to provide reassurance at home.

Marks & Spencer food packaging now tells stories of provenance: where the vegetables were grown, for example, or even the exact location of a farm. It recommends other food or drink to take with a particular meal. And it makes the individual ingredients sound specially chosen because they are described with careful words. This was a style I began with them some years ago, but they have now developed it to a new level. In doing so, they have changed people's minds about how much copy you can actually put on packaging – so 'short' is no longer quite as short as it used to be.

The other aspect of listening is that, as writers, we can all *listen* to improve our writing. I really recommend this. Read your words aloud or inside your head. Do they sound right? Do you need to pause for breath in the wrong places? Are some phrases difficult to say? Do the words flow? If you read your words, you might decide that the answers to some of those questions mean that some rewriting is needed. Go ahead and do it. In time you will enjoy the process. Train your ear – and your inner ear – to listen to the words you've written. It's surprising how often some basic changes in punctuation – a comma added or removed, a full stop to make two sentences out of one, a statement turned into a question – will help your words to sound better and mean more.

It's largely a matter of 'Plain English' – but it goes beyond that. Plain English is like the grammar of writing for business. It provides a solid foundation and it makes sure that people don't sneer at you for your mistakes. But no one said about Shakespeare 'Wonderful writer. Perfect grammar.'

Shakespeare, of course, was particularly conscious of writing to be listened to. In his plays he wrote many of the words in the form of iambic pentameters – where each line of blank verse has five 'feet', an unstressed syllable followed by a stressed one. It was almost the heightened conversational form of his day, or at least his play – an Elizabethan form of rap, providing a structure within which to extemporise. A strict iambic pentameter line might run like this:

The question is to be or not to be.

Except that Shakespeare wrote:

To be or not to be, that is the question.

The breakaway from strict metre, turning around the sentence and putting the question first, puts the line's emphasis on the seemingly insignificant word 'that'. It indicates an element of obsessive thinking, while accentuating the uncertainty in Hamlet's mind. But you need to hear the words not simply read them.

So, the second writing principle that goes with my second record is:

Listen. To your own words as you write. And try to make others listen to your words as if to a wonderful new language.

My third record is *Going underground* by The Jam.

The story behind this is that I wrote a chapter of a previous book *The Invisible Grail* while travelling to work on London Underground. I have always enjoyed the tube for the opportunity to read. A large proportion of the books I have read in my life I have read on the Underground. But I could not think of a book that had been written while travelling on the tube. The idea – picking up on that phrase about 'the fastest way to get from A to B' – was to write a 26-part chapter about writing. The first section would begin with a word beginning with 'A' and would end with a word ending with the letter 'B'. And so on. I called the chapter 'Going underground' because I liked the musical association and it seemed to fit.

I wrote each of the 26 sections working my way from A to B, B to C, through to Y to Z, on my journey to work over a couple of months. In many ways it was the most ridiculous task I've ever given myself. You might imagine that this discipline of starting and ending with certain letters was extraordinarily restrictive and limiting. In fact, in practice, it was amazingly liberating. It meant that each morning, as I got on at Bounds Green on the Piccadilly Line, I had some help to get me started.

'*I need a word beginning with Q*' for example. So I began '*Questions can be very useful in helping you get started on a piece of writing*'. And I was away, I had my subject and now I knew I had to explore that subject and reach a conclusion by the time I got to Covent Garden. And I knew where I was heading: I was making for a word ending in R – which actually gives a lot more choice than the previous section where I'd had to end with a Q. So there was a constraint and it was liberating. Which proved to me again the truth of Douglas R. Hofstadter's words:

> I suspect that the welcoming of constraints is, at bottom, the deepest secret of creativity.

I suggest that you try this yourself. Take a paragraph of writing that you are not happy with. It might be written by you or by someone else in your organisation. You know that it needs rewriting but you are not sure where to start. Give yourself a starting point of a letter – let's say that the first word has to begin with a 'J'. The last word should end with a 'K'. Rewrite the paragraph with those constraints, then try two more combinations of letters to begin and end the paragraph – G to H, for example, and M to N. You will find you are forced, perhaps with surprising enjoyment, into a different tone, probably more conversational.

So the third principle I give you is:

**Set and accept constraints. Welcome them.
Particularly when the constraints are *the brief*.**

My fourth record is Bob Dylan's *Positively 4th Street*. A number
sprang to mind instead of a letter. Sometimes you make
connections by going against an obvious connection. This is a
wonderfully vitriolic song, a rant against someone he didn't like
(some say sections of his audience) and it ends with these words:

> *I wish that for just one time*
> *You could stand inside my shoes*
> *And just for that one moment*
> *I could be you.*
>
> *Yes, I wish that for just one time*
> *You could stand inside my shoes,*
> *You'd know what a drag it is*
> *To see you.*

That is Bob Dylan seeing empathy from a particularly
jaundiced viewpoint. But let's take something positive out of
this. As writers, particularly for organisations that have to try to
understand consumers, we can't afford not to put ourselves in
other people's shoes. And, when you think about it, it's a fairly
fundamental skill for almost any kind of writing. Think of your
reader. Think of your character. Think of your message. Think,
above all: who are you doing this for?

This was how I started when James Hill asked me to help
write the 'Making good better' strategy for Birds Eye Wall's.
I listened to James and others involved. But I thought: who,
in the end, should really benefit from what the company was
doing? Each of us, yes, if we do our jobs better. But, actually,

and more fundamentally, the consumers out there who buy the products and whose lives we can affect by our work. So the starting point for me was to imagine such a consumer and write a very short story about her life. I called her Lisa McNally and this was the story.

> *Lisa McNally had had a hard day at work. She'd had to work an extra hour because money was tight. Then she'd had to pick the kids up from school. They'd had a rotten day too, and they grizzled all the way home. Of course, they were hungry.*

> *Lisa always felt guilty about not cooking 'proper meals' for them. On the way home she stopped at the supermarket to buy something. She bought a frozen meal with ice cream afterwards. When she got home the meal was ready in half an hour. The kids felt better now. But did Lisa?*

There I concentrated on telling a simple tale simply. It seemed to me that the more I embellished it – and that was a temptation – the more manufactured it would seem. So when I talk about 'stories' I'm not necessarily meaning *War and Peace*.

Metaphors can be like tiny stories. Put together a string of metaphors and you can build up a picture of a person you are describing. It's always a useful exercise to think of someone you know well, then to describe that person entirely through metaphors. What kind of animal does (s)he remind you of? A cat, perhaps. But go further than simply 'a cat'. What kind of cat? What colour? What's the cat doing? And often, before you begin a piece of difficult writing, it can be very useful simply to go out for a walk. While walking, look around, take in your surroundings, and bring back an object or a thought that relates in an unusual, metaphorical way to the subject you have to write about. It might be an image of the seagulls swooping for fish, an acorn you pick up in the park or the clock face on the side of a building. The meaning you put on this will help to connect you to a meaning in your reader's life.

The fourth principle I suggest is this:

Put yourself in your reader's place. Imagine the lives of your customers. Show compassion to them.

This is an exercise to try later, but it's more than that. It's almost a requirement of any job – to think of one of your customers as a real person. Ask all the questions you can think of about him or her. Go way beyond the demographic and market research categorisations, find a real individual and build up a portrait of that person. We all write for customers. If you work in HR, your work colleagues are your customers. If you work in finance, operations or IT you will have customers inside the organisation even if your job is not described as 'customer-facing'.

The fifth *Desert Island Disc* is less a record than a performance. One Saturday recently I went to the Barbican to see and hear a performance of *Three Tales* by Steve Reich. This is not my usual choice of music, but we got tickets because it sounded interesting. Steve Reich has been called 'America's greatest living composer'. The piece is electronic, uses a lot of percussion, human voices singing live, and spoken newsreels. And it uses video synchronised to the sound. You had to marvel at the precision timing of everything that happened over the 70 minutes. The three tales were about the uses and abuses of technology: first the Hindenburg airship disaster, then the Bikini atom-bomb explosion, then Dolly the sheep. Words, music, images merged into each other. I'm sorry you will not get the full effect of the images and the sound as well as the words, but imagine fast repetitive music and still images providing a changing background. These words are spoken by a narrator and the radio announcer.

With the Hindenburg tale there was the chilling contrast between the German Ambassador's impassive response: 'It could not have been a technical matter' and the radio announcer's commentary as he watched the airship burst into flames.

'It flashed, it flashed and it's crashing. Bursting, bursting into flame. Oh, it's flames. Get this, get this Scotty! It burst, it burst into flame, into flame. It flashed, it flashed and it's crashing. Oh, it flashed. It's crashing terrible. Get this, get this Scotty.'

[Music stops]

'It could not have been a technical matter.'

Contrast is important in whatever you are writing. Mix short sentences with long ones. Look at the way that, under extreme emotional pressure, the radio announcer achieved almost a form of poetry, using rhymes (perhaps unintentionally), repetitions and variations on set phrases. The words, and the way you place the words, evoke different sounds, emotions and images.

The fifth principle is:

Words appear in a context of sound, vision and memory. Make deliberate use of those associations.

As a child of the sixties, sharing a birthday with George Harrison, I'm still moved by the memory of The Beatles. The sixth record is *Let it be*. My reason for choosing this is that it shows that there is, and needs to be, something almost obsessive about the writing process. That obsession needs to come out in each of us in the form of a commitment to edit our own work.

When *Let it be* was made, the Beatles were breaking up.

They were recording the songs in *Abbey Road* but there were tensions between each of the individuals. Paul McCartney seemed to be the one trying most to hold it all together. Anyway the record company decided that the record could not be finished by the Beatles themselves, so it brought in Phil Spector as producer, and he added string arrangements. That's the version that was issued and that we know.

Paul McCartney later announced that he was going to reissue *Let it be* in a version without strings, closer to the version originally intended by the Beatles. More than 30 years had passed and here was Paul McCartney still wanting to edit his own work. Is it a magnificent or a destructive obsession?

Editing is a skill we all need to cultivate. David Ogilvy, who founded Ogilvy & Mather and was a great writer for business last century, wrote the following:

I'm a lousy copywriter, but I am a good editor.

Of course, he was a great writer too but he gave the credit for that to editing. Good enough for David Ogilvy, good enough for all of us.

When you edit your own work, you really need to engage your brain. The danger is that when you read your own words, you read what you think you've said rather than what you've really said. At the most basic level, this means you don't spot spelling mistakes. And, by the way, there seems to be an acceptance that spelling doesn't matter on emails: 'it's a rough, spontaneous form of communication so sod the spelling'. But the one absolute requirement of any writing – email included – is to be clear. Misspellings introduce confusion if not contusion. You're not being clear, you're not respecting your reader.

So, train yourself to edit what you write. Which means, first, reading your own writing carefully. Then assessing each word, each phrase, each punctuation mark, each sentence, each paragraph. Do they make sense? Will they be clearly understood? Will they achieve your objectives? Can you write something differently? Will that be better? There is always another way of writing something. Try to write in the way that you feel convinced is the most effective for the job you have to do.

So the sixth principle is:

Edit, edit, edit – but know you have to stop.

I was intrigued by this story in the *Guardian*. It was about trying to find a foolproof way to give instructions for flatpack furniture. The *Guardian* sent itself up nicely with the way it wrote the story.

Flatpacks: hate don't just them you

But people assembling the furniture often find the instructions confusing, so they end up putting parts together in the wrong order.

Wait a minute – shouldn't that paragraph go further down the story? Where did I put those instructions?

According to a Swiss technologist, Stavros Antifakos, this kind of mix-up in assembling flatpack furniture, with Shelf A back to front, drawer assembly B jammed against bracket X and dowel F stuck to the cat with wood glue, need no longer happen.

This can be a useful exercise. Take a paragraph of your own writing. A paragraph that you're really not happy with. Is that because, effectively, you've followed the instructions badly and assembled a paragraph from the flatpack that has the door handles on the inside of the wardrobe? (I've done that.) Look at your paragraph as if you've assembled it wrong. What happens, for example, if the second sentence comes before the first? And so on.

The seventh record is *Coney Island* by Van Morrison. Coney Island, I should explain, is a tiny place in the countryside south of Belfast – not the amusement park outside New York.

Coney Island is spoken rather than sung, words with a musical background, and the words describe a Sunday spent travelling in a leisurely way to the place that gives the song its title. It means a lot to me because a colleague got married a few years ago and the wedding was in Belfast, which is her home town. The wedding was great and we stayed an extra day to see something of Northern Ireland. We hired a car, bought the Van Morrison tape because we wanted to play this song in the car and set off to follow the route that autumn Sunday morning. It was one of the most magical days of my life.

I marvel here, with this song, at the power of words to create romantic images with unpromising materials. What Van Morrison does is list – with short but telling embellishments – the different places on the route for this Sunday walk or drive. But, believe me, when you arrive at Coney Island it's an absolute dump. Yet it's not that if you haven't been there. And, even when I've been there, I'm still prepared to go with the overall golden glow of the mood that is created by the words. And the question that ends the song: 'Wouldn't it be great if it was like this all the time?' So when we write, we're writing for people who have never been to Coney Island. But we're trying to make them yearn for it. Use the emotive power of words to create that yearning. Never think 'this can be boring'. Never give yourself that excuse.

For example, what could be more boring than a list? Perhaps you write lists all the time, probably with bullet-points in presentations and documents. Lists that are saying, in effect, 'we've got this, this and this, it's all here, you know what I mean, blah blah blah'.

Well here's a list. It's written as a poem by Maura Dooley. She was commissioned by Polo Mints (watch for the reference), and she called the poem 'What every woman should carry'.

My mother gave me the prayer to St Theresa.
I added a used tube ticket, Kleenex,
several Polo mints (furry), a tampon, pesetas,
a florin. Not wishing to be presumptuous,
not trusting you either, a pack of 3.
I have a pen. There is space for my guardian angel,
she has to fold her wings. Passport.
A key. Anguish at what I said/didn't say
when once you needed/didn't need me. Anadin.
A credit card. His face the last time,
my impatience, my useless youth.
That empty sack, my heart. A box of matches.

I have used that poem as an exercise in workshops. Try it. List the contents of your handbag, briefcase or pockets. Add a few specific details that make them personal, then simply write this as a list. I'm sure you'll find that it's a list with personality. Ask a colleague to write their list and read it. I bet it makes you smile. It makes you warm towards the writer because that writer has expressed something individual that has gone beyond the straightforward provision of information. Can we do that at work? I believe so. You will make your writing more effective by engaging on a human level with the person you are communicating with.

So the seventh principle is:

Transform the most unpromising materials. Not even lists need be boring.

The final record is *Kind and generous* by Natalie Merchant. It's really a simple song. It says 'thank you' and repeats it. We don't say 'thank you' enough. We don't get emotional enough in our writing. We don't put enough of our personalities into our words.

This is a bit of a sad story but I'd like to tell it to make this point. My best friend died two years ago. We'd known each other for 30 years, since we met at university. Mike had been struggling against cancer for the previous five years. At times things seemed fine, but the reality was that he was growing weaker and the cancer was spreading despite all the treatment. He had to give up work as a teacher about two years before he died. He wrote plays and one of them was performed at the Stephen Joseph Theatre, directed by Alan Ayckbourn.

For five years, Mike and I did our best to behave as usual. I didn't really talk to him about the fact that he was dying – it seemed that might precipitate the event. Mike bravely talked about his symptoms, but acted as if he was protecting me from the knowledge we both knew was between us but not spoken. Eventually, a couple of months before he died, I wrote to Mike to say 'thank you'. I explained why he meant so much to me. We later talked on the phone and I know the letter meant a lot to him.

We're humans. Sometimes we seem to be embarrassed to show it. We should try not to be devoid of humanity, even if we're writing for business. Business is all about relationships. Between colleagues. Between companies and suppliers. Between brands and consumers. You need humanity and you need engaging words to develop and maintain relationships.

Here's a company that knows that. Innocent Drinks make smoothies. They started as three young guys who were friends. And they decided to form a business together. They tell their story on their website.

> *In the summer of 1998 when we had developed our first smoothie recipes but were still nervous about giving up our proper jobs, we bought £500 worth of fruit, turned it into smoothies and sold them from a stall at a little music festival in*

London. We put up a big sign saying 'Do you think we should give up our jobs to make these smoothies?' and put out a bin saying 'YES' and a bin saying 'NO' and asked people to put the empty bottle in the right bin. At the end of the weekend the 'YES' bin was full so we went in the next day and resigned.

That's a terrific story. It's an example of the way companies can use storytelling techniques to build their brands. In this case it was about creating a legend, a legend that is totally believable and completely in the spirit of the brand that has since been carried through consistently. The story expresses a fundamental truth about the character of the company.

I found out a lot about Innocent when I wanted to feature them in *The Invisible Grail*. I went over to Fruit Towers in Shepherds Bush, met Richard Reed and his colleagues and I wrote their story as a case study in the book.

Anyway, I sent Richard an email when I finished writing my book. I headed it 'You Smoothies'. Here's the email.

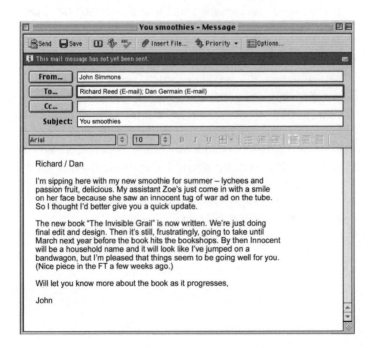

Richard replied in that completely Innocent way, as you can see. 'I think you should leave early tonight and treat yourself to a bottle of wine and sunset to celebrate.'

I'm impressed by the consistency of the Innocent personality, whether it appears on the smoothie bottles, advertising, their vans or emails. Any of these media are seen by them as opportunities to have conversations. And conversations are the most important way we build relationships. Now if all emails were really like conversations perhaps we would press the delete button less quickly.

I decided I should reply to Richard. The header of my reply said 'Out of office reply' – the standard email message when I'm away from the office. But when Richard opened it he read this message:

John Simmons has nipped off home early to treat himself to a bottle of wine and sunset. Thanks for the idea.

To close this email conversation, Richard's message was short:

oh yes.

We always have the option of putting more (or less) of our personality into writing. The starting point for this section was the need to say 'thank you' which is the simplest and commonest expression of emotion in human exchanges. Except that 'thank you' is often said without real emotion, it is hardly more than a clearing of the throat. I often think that 'thank you' is the only phrase you need to find your way easily through everyday transactions, particularly in British shops. We have all been in dialogues that run like this:

'Thank you' – *you put the goods on the counter.*
'Thank you' – *the sales assistant smiles at you and rings*
up the price.
'Thank you' – *you offer your money.*
'Thank you' – *the sales assistant takes your money.*
'Thank you' – *(s)he offers the bag and receipt.*
'Thank you' – *you accept them.*
'Thank you' – *that's it for now.*
'Thank you' – *you both say, in effect, 'goodbye, you've been very*
nice, hope to see you again soon'.

The fact is, that is a perfectly good conversation in a face-to-face situation. At least, we have all experienced much worse, when the sales assistant offers no words at all. Eye contact, our ability to read each other's facial expressions and emphases of tone mean that the communication is reasonably good. But on the written page, or on the computer screen, we cannot expect so much of the reader. We need to reach out and engage with the audience, perhaps especially when we are expressing gratitude. We should all see this as a chance to express more of our own personality – unless we are, by nature, blinkered egomaniacs steeped in a constant attitude of ingratitude. Look for ways to say thank you well.

So the final principle is:

Bring your personality to work. Put it positively into your writing.

Desert Island Discs also allows you to take a book with your eight records. I'm pleased about that. If I were to recommend a final exercise to you, to improve your writing, it would simply be to do more reading. And I'd encourage you to read fiction rather than management books, although a varied diet is always good. Reading really is the flipside of writing. We can learn about writing by reading great writers.

So for my book, I will take an anthology of poetry called *Staying Alive*. (Sounds like another record selection...). It's described as 'real poems for unreal times', 'an anthology of 500 life-affirming poems, helping us to stay alive to the world and stay true to ourselves'.

Here is one of the poems. It's a good example of 'writing short' because it says a lot in 14 lines. But, as E. E. Cummings does, it plays with syntax and it makes you think about the thought by confronting you with an unusual way of speaking it. And, in a strange way, it is a bit like a flatpack poem wrongly assembled but still able to work.

i thank You God for most this amazing
day: for the leaping greenly spirits of trees
and a blue true dream of sky; and for everything
which is natural which is infinite which is yes

(i who have died am alive again today,
and this is the sun's birthday; this is the birth
day of life and of love and wings: and of the gay
great happening illimitably earth)

how should tasting touching hearing seeing
breathing any – lifted from the no
of all nothing – human merely being
doubt unimaginable You?

(now the ears of my ears awake and
now the eyes of my eyes are opened)

The discipline of writing short is an important one. You build up any piece of writing one word at a time. But sometimes you simply go on adding words and, instead of an entrance way, you find you have built an enormous brick wall. Choose each word with care, think about where you are placing it, stand back every so often and assess the pattern of sight, sound and meaning that your words have made. Even the shortest piece of writing can be written in umpteen different ways. There is always another way of looking at things.

Chapter 3
Longer flights of imagination

From short to long. How big a leap is that?

The last chapter was concerned with shorter pieces of writing. Now I want to focus on writing longer pieces. Immediate analogies spring to mind about sprints and marathons, and there is inevitably something daunting in the request to write thousands of words rather than just a few. Despite the old adage about 'I would have written you a shorter letter but I didn't have the time', long documents generally take more time to write than short ones. And, in either case, time is what people always feel short of – or would like to persuade us we are short of. Andrew Marvell used the argument to seduce his 'coy mistress':

Had we but world enough, and time,
This coyness, Lady, were no crime...

But at my back I always hear
Time's winged chariot hurrying near.

So we constantly hear the flapping of wings, not of the dark angels, but the insistency of time. The pressure is to rush. But there is always another pressure, which should be a greater one. We all want to achieve a good outcome, to produce communication that is effective, to meet the objectives we set ourselves or that others set us. Do those objectives always include the legalistic phrase 'time is of the essence'?

When writing a long document you should have time, and you will need time. The important thing will be to manage your time by breaking it down into smaller chunks. If you have two days, two weeks or two months to produce your completed document, you need to plan it and set out clear structural markers along the way. Just as a book has chapters.

CHUNK 1

There are no enormous differences between 'writing short' and 'writing long'. One simply goes on for longer than the other. If you get on a plane and fly from London to Paris, that is not hugely different from the experience of getting on a plane and flying to New York, San Francisco or Tokyo – except for the amount of time involved. But this 'long-haul writing' still needs to use all the principles of writing short that I set out in the previous chapter.

The long flight metaphor seems to work. I will stay with it to guide you through the chapter, itself a demonstration that a metaphor or a theme can help to give structure to a longer piece of writing. But I must also give myself a warning that the overuse of such a theme can become counter-productive. So try to use thematic metaphors lightly; use them only to illuminate meaning.

I have suggested that there is no great difference between writing short and writing long. Long – by which we might mean a business document to make the case for investment, a report to the board, a review of work undertaken by others, whatever – just takes more stamina. But, in fact, the simple trick is that you simply need to see the long pieces as a collection – a properly joined-up collection – of short pieces. Just as a crowd is simply a number of individuals gathered together, a long piece of writing is a number of short pieces put together.

The first page of this chapter took me hours to write. I sat at my desk and spent a couple of hours thinking. Then I got up and took a walk. Much 'writing time' is spent not writing a word. This can be disconcerting, terrifying even, for people who are less used to writing or perhaps even resistant to the task. We all fear the blank page or the blank computer screen. There is no way around it: writer's block can afflict the experienced writer just as much as people who do not classify themselves as writers. Sometimes we simply need to be relaxed about the time that is passing. It's not necessarily writer's block; it's just thinking time. You cannot always force your writing out into the open.

You can, however, try a number of things. A change of scenery can help, and physical exercise of some kind. A long run often helps me think through a piece of writing. But I have to be careful to make notes quickly when I get home so that I don't find myself, like Coleridge, distracted by the intrusion of a sudden awakening from meditation. The man from Porlock knocks: your thoughts rush out of the door as soon as you open it.

You can also make lists. Simply write down points to make or areas to cover. Don't worry at all about how you write these. Put down single words or short phrases. Then pick on one of those words or phrases and start to elaborate it. One way to do this is through automatic writing. As a writer you have the luxury at this stage of not needing to show what you have written to anyone. Take advantage of that. Start with one phrase in your list then continue writing, don't let your pen or pencil leave the page, leave no pauses for thought, just carry on writing without stopping. Carry on like this for ten minutes, or for as long as your wrist can bear it. You will find that you have written a lot of gibberish but you are the only person who will read it, so it really does not matter. Perhaps in there, gleaming among the lines of gibberish, is a thought that you can extract and develop. The important thing is that you will have begun writing. You have moved past the blank page.

CHUNK 2

The hours I spent before writing the opening page had a purpose. For a long-haul flight you need to prepare a bit better and, unfortunately, you probably have to hang around longer at the airport. So what I was really doing before writing the first words was the equivalent of packing my bags, getting myself to the right airport, checking my tickets and passport to make sure I had what I needed, buying a few last-minute things in the airport shops, then sitting in the lounge thinking about the flight and the place I was heading to. And to help me do this, I had a notebook. A notebook that contained snippets of information, thoughts and ideas that I had been collecting for this journey. And that I could also use to start putting down some kind of structure to what I needed to say.

Think of it as the map you refer to, just to check where your flight is taking you.

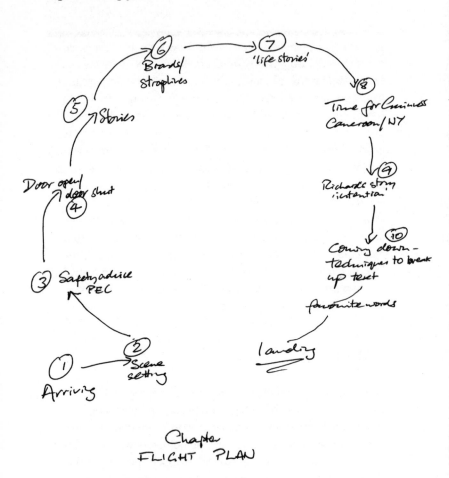

Chapter
FLIGHT PLAN

This is the journey I mapped out. Not the greatest bit of cartography, but I could read it, and that was enough. At this moment, written before I finish writing, I've no idea whether or not I will have stuck to the map by the time I finish this chapter. The importance of this kind of map is that it gives you an idea of where you are heading but, because you are the pilot, you can ignore its detail if something unforeseen (such as a completely new thought) comes along to change your course.

CHUNK 3

Anyway, it's time to get on board. The real journey starts here, with some first words from novels. In each case I invite you to consider the way the words achieve their effects and to wonder if a similar approach might work for your next piece of long business writing.

It was a bright cold day in April, and the clocks were striking thirteen.
[1984]

We all like to be arrested by an opening. The need with first lines is to engage quickly with your readers. You might do this by putting something unexpected into the completely conventional – like the clocks striking 13 in George Orwell's opening to *1984*. For example: *Last financial year was out of the ordinary: we tried, but failed, to make a profit.*

Call me Ishmael.
[Moby-Dick]

Herman Melville throws down a challenge in the opening three words of his novel. It makes you pause but be prepared for the flow of words that will follow. It almost has the quality of an advertising strapline or the shout line on a film poster. Could your report do something similar? For example, if writing a case to the board of Nike, would it begin like this: *Just do it.* The three-word sentence can be useful as a way to demand attention. Try it occasionally. It usually works.

> *The first time I laid eyes on Terry Lennox he was drunk in a Rolls-Royce Silver Wraith outside the terrace of The Dancers.*
> [The Long Goodbye]

Raymond Chandler plunges you into the middle of things in a different way, with a different tone. Here it's all about setting the scene, involving you in the milieu of spoilt hedonistic characters. It's also written in the first person, using the narrator's memory of a first impression. Is this very different from a business example like: *When I first came across this company I wanted to buy it?*

> *Which road this afternoon, madam?*
> [The Twyborn Affair]

Patrick White's opening uses a question that opens a conversation. It establishes that there are two people in the scene and the conversation. Questions can be very effective openings to longer pieces of writing. Perhaps your question sets out, in a relatively informal way, the subject you are asking your readers to address and decide upon. Through its attitude it might set out clearly the direction of your argument. For example: *Can we afford not to invest in our future?*

> *What is time? We ascended towards the light, five floors up, and split up into thirteen rows facing the god who unlocks the gates of morning.*
> [Borderliners]

Peter Hoeg's opening also uses a question but in a more philosophical, less conversational way. Here the question is internal, the writer is meditating with himself. He goes on from the question into a scene that seems to place us into a context of surreal storytelling. Business storytelling can rarely venture into the surreal, but it can aim to seize attention with similar techniques. For example: *Are we serious about the environment? Last year we produced tons of waste that we failed to recycle. This year we must do better.*

Those first lines are all from novels, of course, and you will be writing business reports. Business reports that sometimes start like this.

Project type: Roll out
Project start date: 15/01/04
Project leader: Jonathan K
Category: Ice cream
Target launch date: 12/10/04
Launch date status: Confirmed
Strategic intent: Platform

The opening there really is like the freight manifest, a plain inventory of factual information. The first actual sentence is this.

Ordinarily for Charter Gate purposes information would only be required under the headings with an asterisk (*). When saved, the title of this form will automatically appear in the calendar.

Of course, a form is not an emotive piece of writing. So I suppose forms are constructed to ensure consistency across different projects, to make them easy to fill in quickly and, for those reading them, easy to extract relevant messages from.

But I wonder. I wonder if we could do more. Because the real purpose of the form I have used as an example is to enthuse people with the excitement of a new product launch. People reading it can contribute energy to the objective of a successful launch. Do these forms, the basis of long written documents, enable energy and enthusiasm to be generated?

Here are the opening lines describing the 'Project Idea'.

To launch 'Magic Moments' – a new bite-size Magic product containing 18 x 12ml bite-size pieces of Magic chocolate covered ice-cream, each piece containing one of three different indulgent centres. The alternative indulgent centres are caramel, chocolate and hazelnut.

As an alternative, could we have an opening line that went something like this?

We think people will love bite-size chunks of different flavoured ice-cream covered in chocolate.

Have I cheated? Probably. But I go back to some of the things I was suggesting in the previous chapter. Don't give yourself the excuse – 'this can be boring'. Even if you're writing a list, it *can* be made interesting as we showed in 'writing short'. And, in terms of 'writing long', the principle of trying to make each sentence 'charged with meaning' is absolutely valid. Sentence by sentence you construct a paragraph. Make sure each sentence means something. Paragraph by paragraph you create a longer document. Make sure each paragraph has the effect of making your reader want to read the next one.

I don't want to belabour the point about the importance of opening lines and first words. And often, in fact, the first words are written much later, when you really know what you have said and you want to summarise it. That is perfectly valid; indeed it's an essential part of the editing process. Why I think the first words that you see or hear really matter, whether they're written first or last, is that they establish the tone of your document. They give a sense of expectation: this will be interesting or boring, I need to read this, I want to read this – or I'll skip through it and get the drift.

CHUNK 4

So we're about to take off. We've thought about what we need to say, we've plotted a map that sets out the main events along the way, and we've started – in our heads – to give a lot of attention to what the first words will be. We also need some basic ground rules before we fly, the equivalent of the Safety Demonstration. Let's make sure that the way we write will not lead to any disturbance, confusion or loss of attention by our readers. The Plain English Code is as good a safety guide as any.

I will:
- *match my writing to the needs and knowledge of the readers, remembering that many of them will be baffled by official jargon and procedures;*
- *consider carefully the purpose and message before starting to write, remembering that clear writing can only stem from clear thinking;*
- *structure the document clearly, perhaps with lists, headings and a pithy summary of key points;*
- *try to write sentences that average 15–20 words;*
- *try to keep the word order simple by putting the doer early in the sentence and following it with an active voice verb;*
- *take pride in everyday English, sound grammar and accurate punctuation;*
- *use 'I', 'we' and 'you' to make the writing more human;*
- *maintain the flow by starting some sentences with link words like 'but', 'however', 'so' and 'because';*
- *use commands when writing instructions;*
- *cut verbiage (at this particular moment in time);*
- *tell customers and colleagues clearly, concisely and courteously what has happened, how the situation stands, and what they can expect next;*
- *test high-use documents with typical users.*

As with the Safety Demonstration on a plane, we probably have a tendency not to bother to listen – or at least to nod or smile at the attendants just to reassure them that we understand this perfectly. But it's worth taking most of this to heart. I particularly like 'tell customers and colleagues clearly, concisely and courteously what has happened, how the situation stands, and what they can expect next'. Next we'll look at some useful advice from Stephen King.

In his book *On writing*, Stephen King describes how, as a difficult school student, he was channelled towards a career in journalism. He was given an offer he couldn't refuse and joined the local newspaper as a sports reporter. The paper editor, John Gould, quickly proceeded to edit Stephen King's first piece of journalism. The process looked brutal – lots of crossing out, lots of rewriting – but it was a revelation for the young writer.

> 'When you write a story, you're telling yourself the story,' he said. 'When you rewrite, your main job is taking out all the things that are not the story.'

> Gould said something else that was interesting on the day I turned in my first two pieces: write with the door closed, rewrite with the door open. Your stuff starts out being just for you, in other words, but then it goes out. Once you know what the story is and get it right – as right as you can, anyway – it belongs to anyone who wants to read it.

There are a lot of important points there, and the advice to 'write first with the door closed, then with the door open' was something I'd never come across before. I think it can apply to business writing, perhaps even more than to fiction. What I'm interested in, for all of us, is to see how far we can challenge ourselves, how far we can stretch ourselves to produce writing that goes beyond the conventional standards of business communications. One way to do that is simply to try, with your first draft, 'writing with the door closed': in other words, no one else is going to read it, it's just for you so don't be held back by those thoughts like 'that's not the way we do things here'. For example, try the automatic writing exercise that I suggested earlier. The editing possibilities should be obvious with this writing, so set about making sense of what you have written. Look at the punctuation, the construction of your sentences, meaning and order, listen to what you have written, make it sound better.

But, of course, we are all – and rightly so – brought back to this question: 'Who is the reader? Who is this aimed at?' And we need to keep our awareness of that reader's needs – and of the possibilities we have to surprise and engage the reader. So we are ready to write 'with the door open', to expose our work to other readers.

CHUNK 5

The switch from the Plain English Campaign to Stephen King is a sign of where my advice is heading. Plain English has its feet firmly on the ground; it's useful but our writing will not soar to any great heights as a result of taking it to heart. I would much rather you took the idea of storytelling to your heart. That will give you more emotion to inspire your business writing.

The heart decides, the mind confirms. That's really how you get through to people. Don't ever believe we're primarily rational creatures. We're dark angels: we have known reason but we have chosen to follow our emotions. We make decisions on the basis of emotions, and we use facts and evidence to support the decisions our emotions are pointing us towards. 'Come, gather round, I'll tell you a story' is an irresistible temptation for us. And it works just as well when you are writing for business, whether your story is contained in a short paragraph or developed into a full report.

'That's how people live, Milt' – Michael Antoniou again, still
kindly, gently – *'by telling stories. What's the first thing a kid*
says when he learns how to talk? "Tell me a story." That's how
we understand who we are, where we come from. Stories are
everything.'

[Jeffrey Eugenides, Middlesex]

Clearly storytelling is at the heart of human identity. But
storytelling is also at the heart of the identity of any company
or brand. Sometimes, though, it has been buried deep under
layers of bureaucracy, management-speak or incomprehension.
Increasingly, brands are recognising that they need to find
and express their individual stories to connect more effectively
with customers inside and outside the company. This is a case
I argued in *The Invisible Grail* and others are making the same
case from different viewpoints.

It means that brands have become interested in language.
Owners and managers of brands are now asking questions of
their verbal identity that they used to ask only of their visual
identity. What is our language saying about us as a brand? Is it
representing our values well? Does it express our personality?
There is always a desire, in the business world, to codify in
order to understand and manage better the assets you have
identified. But what elements of language can a brand actually
'own' in the way that it owns a logo?

CHUNK 6

A brand can certainly own a name, and it can even back its
ownership with legal protection. Sometimes it can own a
phrase because it enters popular consciousness after repeated
advertising. In recent years we have examples like 'Whassup'
for Budweiser or 'Have it … oh yes' for John Smith's beer. But
these are phrases that capture a particular moment in popular
culture as part of an advertising campaign. In ten years' time

those phrases will conjure up a nostalgic memory of the early years of this century. In terms of ownership (legal or moral), they so enter the public consciousness that the original connection to the brand gets stretched. You no longer knew, or needed to know, that 'whassup' derived from Budweiser advertising by the time it had spread by word of mouth, from comic sketch to pub conversation.

Do straplines have more value to the brand? Do they last longer? Let's take 'Just do it' or 'Think different' as examples. These have become essential components of the brand identities of Nike and Apple, and there are many other examples of straplines associated with brands. But even straplines are relatively generic: it's only the power of repetition that attaches 'Just do it' specifically to Nike. Even though the line fits Nike's personality perfectly it could easily have been attached to, say, Coca-Cola with a similar application of media clout. It's the quintessential strapline of a modern brand that offers, by association, an aspirational connection to motivate its consumers. Its universality explains why it has been so widely imitated and also why the plethora of other brand straplines lack real distinctiveness.

What it comes down to is that a brand can 'own' only its own stories. These have been created by the unique events that have happened to or been triggered by the brand and by its significant characters. Yet very few brands have recorded or valued their stories in modern times, perhaps because people felt 'history' was not appropriate to contemporary marketing. Or, perhaps because people feel 'stories just happen', no one in the company managed every detail of that story. People in business like to seem good managers: they like to feel in control. Stories are beyond the control of management. They are too unpredictable a resource to be managed.

There is one exception to this – the founder's story. The Internet has enabled every company and every brand to tell the story of its origins whereas previously the accusation of 'over-weaning pride' (the vice of the fallen angels) had held companies back from elaborating stories that had to be expensively printed. To take one area, coffee: Nescafé, Folgers and Maxwell House all now tell their founding stories on their websites. They are not particularly absorbing stories but at least telling them shows that these big brands have a sense of corporate memory.

Try it for your own organisation. How was it first founded? Who were the people involved? What were their motivations? Is there a demonstration in this story of the values that now drive your organisation? At the most mundane level, companies (particularly professional consultancies) record case studies of previous work. Such case studies can be transformed by imaginative storytelling, giving attention to plot, characters and narrative theme.

CHUNK 7

At a more philosophical level, every brand must have a story, one that can be called its 'life story'. Successful brands work by their ability to bring people together. The more we move into a networking world, the more true this becomes. Think of Starbucks, for example, with its idea of being the 'third place' between work and home – creating a social meeting place. Amazon with its links: 'People who bought this also bought this'. Microsoft with its thought: 'Where do you want to go today?' And certainly Google, whose name has become a verb for the process of making fast, accurate and surprising connections.

If a brand has a story – embedded in its reason for being – it must connect, or wish to connect, with people's lives. This is the real purpose of a brand. So there needs to be, at the heart of any brand, a story about the effect it wishes to have on life and people's lives. A brand like Coca-Cola is now very clear about this.

Coca-Cola isn't a drink. It's an idea. Like great movies, like great music. Coca-Cola is a feeling.

Coca-Cola is refreshment and connection. Always has been … always will be. We're headed to ideas. Ideas that bring entertainment value to our brands, and ideas that integrate our brands into entertainment.

We're moving to ideas that elicit emotion and create connections.
[Steven J. Heyer, Chief Operating Officer, the Coca-Cola Company, 2003]

The word Steven Heyer does not use is 'story', but it is implied in everything he says. Some might argue that he knows the theory but not the practice of storytelling, yet Coca-Cola continues to make connections with people's lives. It is clearly more than a fizzy brown liquid. Like all stories it has a transformational potential.

The life story of a brand, its central narrative theme, describes how and why the brand enables change from one condition to another. For the UK lottery operator, Camelot, this might be expressed as: 'A small investment brings hope of transformation from an ordinary life to an extraordinary one'. A brand like Guinness might express its life story as: 'In a world that's increasingly complex and confusing, Guinness gives you the inner strength to bring greater certainty and simplicity to your life'.

It is vital for any brand to get its life story clear. It does not really matter if it is called the life story, essence, idea or narrative theme. What matters is that it identifies the effect that the brand has, or intends to have, on people's lives. This then creates the framework within which all the brand's stories can be told.

CHUNK 8

Let me stay with Guinness because it is a brand I know well. It is an iconic brand, much better loved than the product itself that remains at the core of the brand. Indeed in many parts of the world – South Africa is one example – Guinness plays in its advertising on the fact that so many people dislike the beer's taste. Billboards there, using market research figures, proclaim: '0.34% of beer drinkers can't be wrong' and 'Joe Bloggs hated it'. The message is 'Guinness is an acquired taste'. The advertising appealed to the customers' sense of individuality, playing to the brand essence of 'Guinness reflects your inner strength'.

Guinness came to a realisation in 2004 that it spoke about the 'essence' in two different ways. In more recent years, as it worked to refine and define its brand, it has increasingly used the word essence in the context of the brand. But since the early 1960s Guinness has had another essence, a product essence. This is Guinness Flavour Extract, GFE, a pure, concentrated essence of Guinness that is used to provide consistent flavour, colour and bite to every Guinness that is drunk anywhere in the world. In effect, this is Guinness's secret ingredient, enabling it to brew Guinness not just in Ireland but in nearly 50 countries around the world.

I was asked to write a book of stories that would unite these two ideas of 'essence': the product and the brand. The narrative theme of inner strength set the framework for the stories. But how could I approach this?

I decided that I would use the archetypal story of the quest. The quest would be to find the real essence of Guinness. I needed characters: a narrator who would be an innocent abroad, in search of the essence, drawing on the help of his inner resources and of other characters encountered along the way. The plot would involve the central character travelling to twelve different countries in a round-the-world journey, before returning to Dublin. By the time he returned, as a result of the wisdom gained from his experiences in the different places, the

narrator would have a deeper knowledge of the brand essence
– and would be entrusted with the product essence too.

This worked for Guinness. I set twelve different themes to
explore through the twelve stories; the themes were all aspects
of inner strength. For example, here is the story set
in Cameroon.

You step off the plane and it's like stepping into a steam
bath. I'd flown in from Paris and now here I was in Douala,
Cameroon.

'Avancez,' was the instruction.

'Keep moving forward' was the way I translated it to myself. I
joined the queue of people making for the arrivals hall and the
baggage carousel. 'Avancez, avancez.'

So that's what I did, through passport control, baggage hall and Customs. 'What's the purpose of your visit?'

'Guinness,' I replied.

'Avancez.'

An unbelievable jostle of people, all competing for a share of my custom. But I'd already declared my purpose. 'Guinness,' I said, and the taxi driver smiled.

He drove me at a speed that seemed more than the car or the road could live with. But he kept going through the blackness outside while my knuckles clenched white inside. The journey was short and fast.

Downtown Douala was teeming with people, noise and colour.

I paid the driver, stepped out onto the road and straight into the bar. My eyes couldn't take in the mixture of blazing light and murky dark, but my legs kept me moving forward. I wasn't sure where I was heading but I knew what I had to do. At the back, in the heaving throng, I found the counter and the barman. He took the cap off the bottle for me, my first Guinness Foreign Extra Stout. A big bottle, it seemed to speak with a voice of power.

Drink, it said. Enjoy. The foreign will soon seem familiar.
Keep moving forward.

The narrator travels from Ireland to the UK, France, Cameroon, Nigeria, South Africa, Singapore, Australia, Japan, Canada, USA, Jamaica and back to Ireland. Each chapter has a different theme which is explored through a story of a few hundred words. So the starting point is a few words – *Be true to yourself*, for example, or *Keep your focus* – that grow into a short story; but each story is part of a longer narrative of a few thousand words. Writing long really is the result of many examples of writing short.

Here is a useful exercise to try for yourself. There is a skill in the writing of epigrams – short, pithy sayings . 'Patriotism is the last refuge of the scoundrel', for example. Think about a word that seems to have a special resonance in your organisation. It might be an adjective like 'natural' or a noun like 'discovery'. Write a series of epigrams that incorporate that word. Work at it for a while until you have a list of, say, twenty epigrams. One of them might have a special meaning for you and your company. It could provide the narrative theme for a brand story.

CHUNK 9

Theme is vital. It sets the objective for your storytelling. You might find it hard to think of report writing as storytelling, but the best way to write an effective report is to tell a good story. The same principles apply. You will have a plot, the message you have to convey. There will be characters, not least yourself, the author. And there should be a theme, which you might prefer to express as the objective. Whether your communication is short or long, the most important thing is to be clear about your objective. It's worth spending time thinking through the objective of your communication.

A useful insight into the importance of setting clear objectives comes from the theatrical world. Richard Hahlo runs workshops at the National Theatre and for a wide variety of businesses, using dramatic techniques to explore issues of communication. This goes way beyond 'presentation skills' as his book *Dramatic Events* makes clear. There is one exercise he describes that has a particular relevance to this chapter. In this exercise he asks three people to improvise a scene at breakfast – involving three characters, Louise, Martin and Natalie. The three are asked to talk about breakfast and nothing but breakfast – no other subjects are allowed.

The 'actors' improvise a short scene around the inevitable toast, marmalade, bacon and eggs, coffee and tea. Then the workshop leader takes Louise aside and asks her to convey that she is in love with Martin, and wanting to tell him so. But still she is only allowed to talk about breakfast.

The second improvisation becomes much more charged. The observers are asked to comment on what they see. They understand that something new has been added to the improvisation's basic diet of tea and toast. The audience becomes much more engrossed in this second version. The element that has been added is that Louise has been given an objective – to communicate her love for Martin. It becomes much more interesting to watch someone pursuing a clear purpose.

The same principles apply to writing, including business writing. Be clear about your objective. What is it that you are trying to achieve? Who are you trying to persuade? Everything you write should work towards the achievement of that objective. If so you will find your readers more involved, just as the audience becomes more involved in the breakfast improvisation when an objective is introduced.

CHUNK 10

I have taken literally my advice to break a long document down into chunks – in the case of this chapter, ten chunks that I have simply numbered to draw attention to the technique. I could have given the ten chunks more descriptive headings, perhaps relating to the long-haul metaphor. *Setting out* through to *Touching down*. But the metaphor would have been strained and there is another point I was attempting to make.

Headings are useful to guide the reader through a longer piece of writing. They have a function, like the overhead signs at an airport: they tell you where you are going and where you need to go. But headings have another purpose that is much simpler and more basic. They provide the reader with a time and place to pause, rest and think. And if the reader cannot finish the reading of a document at one sitting, headings also supply a recognisable place to stop. This means that the heading can be more important for its purpose – to provide a pause – than for the meaning it conveys in its words. 'Chunk 1' through to 'Chunk 10' allows the reader to understand clearly where a pause can best be taken.

There are other ways, within a longer piece of writing, of achieving similar effects. Paragraphs have the same purpose, but they are less obvious invitations to pause. Sometimes it can be enough to introduce an extra line space, or a row of asterisks.

* * *

Sometimes a chart, an illustration, a table or a photograph will help to break up dense text.

The important point, when writing a long document, is to be aware of the needs of your reader. You cannot write just for yourself. You need to have a real audience in mind. Warren E. Buffett, the American financial analyst, has his sister Doris in mind when he writes about investment matters. If you cannot think of who your audience might be, he invites you to borrow Doris.

There is a serious point that Buffett is making. Too many people who write about finance, or business more generally, forget that communication is between two individuals. Both individuals are human beings. Respect each other's humanity, be compassionate in your communication, think about your reader's needs and your own needs. Aim to increase the amount of enjoyment that you get from writing the document, and that your reader will get from reading it.

I was recently asked by D & AD (Design & Art Direction) to answer the following question in fewer than 25 words: 'What does creativity mean to you?' My reply was the following:

It's being curious about what you take out of life and being
passionate about what you put into it.

This is summed up for me in an exercise that begins with the question: 'What is your favourite word?' Animated discussion take place in groups about the relative merits of custard, pitter-patter, oxymoron and debacle – examples of words that have developed personal significance to people. From this point people are invited to construct an idea for a product or a brand, a company or a service. Within a short time, spurred by a single word, plausible concepts for new businesses are being described.

Ask yourself, what is your favourite word? Tomorrow perhaps
you will change your mind; another day, another word. That is
perfectly fine. All I suggest is the possibility that you might have a
special feeling towards a particular word. We can give individual
words respect and love and a special place in our minds.

Words are our children. We need to look after them; they thrive on the care and interest we give them. Each word matters, and you construct language by adding one word to another. We need to care about each and every one of those words when we use them, we need to care about the order in which we set them. But it all starts with the potential of individual words.

This chapter has been about 'writing long'. The longest journey starts with the first step. Each word has a role to play in creating a piece of writing – long or short – that is engaging and effective. So build up your long pieces by giving every bit as much attention to the principles of 'writing short'.

We return to the long-haul metaphor, about to land in the place that is our destination. For me that place is where I write, it is London, a city of several million individuals. From the window they are indistinguishable, except as points of light, but I know that they are there, as soon as I can get closer. Those individuals live in different parts of the city that are like individual villages. Together they make the whole.

Think of your words as individuals.

Chapter 4
Art and myth, word and image

This chapter describes a recent but very unusual project. It's very rare, as a writer for business, to be given a brief that is completely open. *Create a work of art*, that was the brief. *A work that we can display in our offices.*

Having stressed the creative advantages of a brief – the challenge it provides to work against constraints – the lack of constraints in this assignment was daunting. It came from Lever Fabergé, a Unilever company in Kingston in south-west London. Here for the last few years Alastair Creamer has been producer of the Catalyst programme, which aims to increase the creativity of Unilever's people through working with artists of many different kinds. I had had a number of involvements with the programme, principally during a six-month period when I was 'creative business writer in residence' alongside the poet Jackie Wills.

Now, at the beginning of 2003, the ten artists who had been most involved in the work of Catalyst, were invited to make a work of art inspired by one of Lever Fabergé's brands. I was pleased to be counted as an artist and invited to participate with people like Helen Storey, the concept artist and fashion designer, and Andy Sheppard, the jazz saxophonist. Others were painters, photographers, poets.

Catalyst is an extraordinary programme, unlike anything I have come across in the business world: brave, ambitious and almost romantically optimistic. Yet it is measured by hard business criteria, and it works – so much so that the programme spread from Lever Fabergé to Birds Eye Wall's and to other companies inside and outside Unilever. Business is becoming serious about creativity.

The brief each of us was given was simple. There were no written instructions: we were simply supplied with the products of one Lever Fabergé brand. Helen Storey, for example, was assigned to Persil, the washing powder; Andy Sheppard was given Vaseline. My brand was Dove, deodorant and personal care products for women.

Each of us was asked to keep a diary to record our thoughts during the making of the work. This was a useful task. I doubt if I would have been as disciplined if I had not been asked to keep this diary. It provided me with the constraints I needed to work against, giving me the medium to explore my thinking. In this chapter I reproduce my words from that diary, without editing, because those raw words shine some light on the creative process.

My main fear was that the 'art' was intended to be displayed. The requirement to keep a diary was reassuring because it was obviously to do with words. For some of the other artists, the diary was probably more daunting than the creation of a painting or a photograph. I felt confident about producing words. But how could those words be displayed in Lever Fabergé's new reception area or offices in a way that would look at all interesting to an employee or a visitor? Would I be pushed towards creating a work in a medium that would not be close to my expertise? Yet I felt that words and images had always been close collaborators in my work. I had worked with designers throughout my career. That was a thought I kept in mind as I began thinking about the project and writing the diary that makes up the rest of this chapter.

* * *

DOVE DIARY

15 JANUARY 2003

Lunch with Alastair and Matt to talk about the commission. My brand is Dove – a G6, i.e. global brand. It's exciting but I suspect it will become increasingly daunting as this goes on. The meaning of the complete openness of the brief will creep up on me.

*

Woke in the middle of the night and was thinking about the commission. I'm sure there's an expectation that I will do something based around words. Should I resist that or go with it? To be fair, there's no pressure from Lever Fabergé either way.

*

Two thoughts. First, it would be good to produce a rug. Rugs can be beautiful. Can words be woven into them? Can the rug be a bathmat? Or even after Magritte, 'this is not a bathmat'. Or 'Always make sure you're clean.'

Second thought, what does Dove mean in other languages? It's Italian for 'Where?' Gauguin painting – 'Where do we come from? Where are we going?'

*

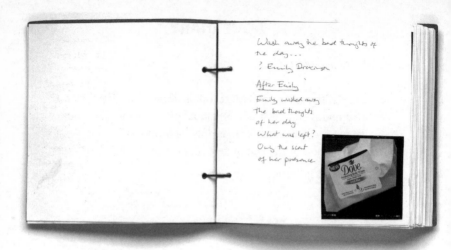

Wash away the bad thoughts of the day...

? Emily Dickinson

After Emily
Emily washed away
the bad thoughts
of her day.
What was left?
Only the scent
of her presence.

*

The box finally turned up. It had been delivered on Christmas Eve, then taken up to the fourth floor where it had stayed in Smythe DL's reception 'waiting for someone to claim it'.

Anyway it turned up in my office on Friday 17th – I unpacked it, an enormous box with the Dove symbol. Inside, eventually, like the Russian doll box, was a cardboard box containing Dove products, the brief and half a dozen boards.

*

Water – images seen through water. Can glass add to that effect? A glass box within which an image sits.

Or a large piece of glass with a magnifying lens set within it – through the glass you read words.

I like the idea of different layers, like seeing people through water, because Dove seems fundamentally to go with water.

*

The name Emily seems to me a very feminine one – and very Dove-like. There's almost a hesitation talking about feminine or femininity, as if it's not quite PC. But I guess there aren't many men buying Dove for its masculinity.

So femininity is OK. What would be the image of femininity? That might be a Dove image.

It's different from girl/girlie/girlishness on the one hand – or woman/womanly on the other. And very different from ladylike.

*

Emily Dickinson. I keep coming back to this thought. Just a memory that there is something in her poetry that is quintessentially feminine, but the memory might be false. Her poems are very small, in line length and volume of words. About seeing small details as representative of universalities – the small in the big, the big in the small.

*

18 JANUARY

Three Colours.
White, Blue and Blue.

Looking at a collection of Dove products there's a colour consistency of the three colours – all aimed at projecting a clean image. The white is obvious. But the interplay of Blue and Blue is interesting. There's gold there too for the Dove symbol, a highlight.

*

Two DVDs given to me as Christmas presents. Marlene Dietrich in *The Blue Angel* and Juliette Binoche in *Three Colours Blue*.

Seeing *The Blue Angel* again, Dietrich is surprisingly plump
– definitely womanly. Juliette Binoche, though, is wonderfully
feminine. She could be the face of Dove.
Both films, in memory at least, have a blue tinge over them
– not so much black and white as blue and white.

*

By a piece of serendipity I found this silver sequin on the sofa
I'm sitting on. From one of our Indian cushion covers probably.
It landed on one of the Dove images 'Concept: Water'. Is this
suggesting something? I quite like the thought of a glittering
photo. Like the after-effect of one of those Lush 'Bath
Ballistics' – glitter on skin, changing as the light changes.

*

Can you mix glitter into the photographic development
process? Leaving a sheen on the shining of an image. Or
words that you read – like silver blocking on a book cover
– silver from one side, grey from another.

Perhaps the words – a poem – could be overlaid on an
image? Perhaps you can only read the silver words in certain
light, or seen from the side?

*

19 JANUARY

Decided to pursue the Emily Dickinson thought a bit further,
to see where it leads, if anywhere. Looked up her life in the
Oxford Companion. Sounds sad – 'she never told her love'.
A solitary life, led indoors, not seeing people, an inner life,
devoted to writing poems (some 2,000) only seven of which
were published (heavily edited) in her lifetime. She wrote in
packets of 'fascicles' which were discovered after her death.

There's something here in the essence of life being captured in little packets or packages.

*

My immediate and lingering response to the Dove collection sent to me is that this is about femininity. And I suppose I instinctively associated an idea of femininity with an idea of Emily Dickinson. 'Ideas' because I'm not sure I really know them, don't really have definitions of them in my head.

So, pursuing Emily Dickinson, it's interesting to pick up a volume of poems from my book shelf. It's called 'Taking off Emily Dickinson's clothes' by Billy Collins.

*

Here's part of the Billy Collins' poem 'Taking off Emily Dickinson's clothes'.

> *Then the long white dress, on more*
> *complicated matter with mother-of-pearl*
> *buttons down the back,*
> *so tiny and numerous that it takes forever*
> *before my hands can part the fabric,*
> *like a swimmer's dividing water,*
> *and slip inside.*

Particularly in the last three lines there is something of Dove, an image to hold on to, the seamlessness of water after discarding the seams of human clothing.

> [Funnily enough there was also a Billy Collins connection to Lever Fabergé – Jackie Wills used his poem 'Introduction to poetry' as part of our residency.]

Then from Emily Dickinson herself, the following poem:

> *I think that the root of the Wind is Water –*
> *It would not sound so deep*
> *Were it a Fundamental Product –*
> *Airs no Oceans keep –*
> *Mediterranean intonations –*
> *To a Current's Ear –*
> *There is a maritime conviction*
> *In the Atmosphere –*

The image in the back of my mind contains the following
elements:
>   a young woman
>   blue colours
>   rippling water
>   glittering stars
>
>   From stars we come
>   to stars we go

Like the Emily Dickinson, not a 'Fundamental Product' – to
do with Air and Water, not Earth and Fire.

25 JANUARY

To do this I need the help of Jessie, my daughter, because
I'm talking about a photograph.

Perhaps with a glimpse of words beneath the surface.

Or perhaps with some words overlaid.

Or perhaps the words are separated completely, placed on the frame.

*

One of the exercises I did with the Lever Fabergé Deodorants team during my Catalyst residency was the Metaphor exercise – 'He is/she is' etc.

I should do it myself on Dove,

Colour
Vehicle
Object
Plant
Time of day
Place
Sounds

So here goes

She is the blue where the sky meets the sea.
She is the mermaid gliding through the waters.
She is the seashore, forever changing,
as the tide washes away the form she had taken.
She is a flower that grows among
the rock pools where the salty sun shines.
She is always there, from morning
to midnight and onwards.
She is a Mediterranean island set in a blue sea.
She is the gentlest lapping of the waves
              on a sandy shore.

*

SUNDAY

Thoughts on the run, come back to these later.

A lingering thought

Ablution is the preparation for Absolution

Deification of a woman. Something religious in the idea of
washing, reflect mythologies. From the Greek/Roman myths.
Botticelli's Venus rising from the foam.
Dove vene Dove?

*

Dove and water go together

Da dove viene Dove?

The correct Italian version from Marianna.

Where does Dove come from?

*

What I'm after is a new visual representation of the creation
of a goddess. A goddess representing femininity – not
necessarily love – but the thought is inseparable from the
Botticelli *Birth of Venus*. It's inescapable, it's so well known
so that, even without looking at it again, I see in my mind
the naked figure of Venus in the scallop shell, rising from the
foaming sea.

*

So (1 Feb) I looked up a book of classical myths to see if there were any further clues. And the serendipitous trail continues…

*

> *Aphrodite, Goddess of Desire, rose naked from the foam of the sea and, riding on a scallop shell, stepped ashore first on the island of Cythera…Grass and flowers sprang from the soil wherever she trod.*
>
> *Some say that she sprang from the foam… that Zeus begot her on Dione, daughter of Air and Earth. But all agree she takes the air accompanied by doves and sparrows'*
> [The Greek Myths]

*

'Aphrodite means "foam-born".'

The goddess has close associations with the sea.

'Accompanied by doves …' It's the final nod of the head, the go-ahead. This must be the image. A new goddess, not of love but of femininity, must be born.

*

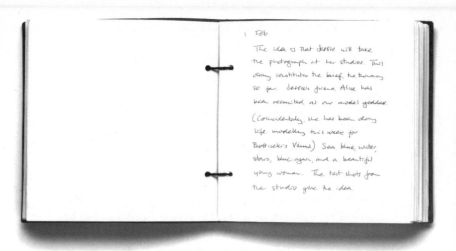

1 FEBRUARY

The idea is that Jessie will take the photograph at her studios. This diary constitutes the brief, the thinking so far. Jessie's friend Alice has been recruited as our model goddess. (Coincidentally, she has been doing life modelling this week for Botticelli's Venus). Sea, blue, water, stars, blue again, and a beautiful young woman. The test shots from the studio give the idea.

*

There's not quite enough mystery yet. The colour seems just right. 'She is the blue where the sky meets the sea.'

Jessie has really interesting idea, to make a triptych. I like this because it can be more mysterious, and it suggests a religious context that I've always felt should be implied.

*

Time to write a myth, the birth of Dove

Some say that Aphrodite never fell in love, but that everyone who saw her fell in love with her. The gods knew the truth. Aphrodite had fallen in love with the God of Clouds and she was never able to love another. Aphrodite melted into his embrace, but he vanished into the air and never again was Aphrodite able to find the shape and texture that she loved. The child of this fleeting union was Dove.

Dove was born one morning at the blue horizon. Those who had seen Aphrodite pass by went in pursuit of the goddess, driven by their hopeless love, but none of them could reach the horizon. Like Aphrodite herself, it remained forever out of reach.

Where the sky met the sea, Dove was born. Her bed was a rock pool, her lullaby was the lapping water, her playthings were the stars. Her birth-gift from her mother was eternal maturity; she was born a woman and she never aged after the day of the birth. The gift from her father was a blanket of sea mist, which kept her hidden from the gaze of men.

There she dwells still, never ageing, never seen, waiting for the day when her mother will rediscover her father. On that day she will be free to go her own way and find her own love. So she sits and waits for the golden dove to appear, Aphrodite's messenger that will bring the longed-for news.

*

14 FEBRUARY

Talked to Alastair. Reception opening 11 April. Need to aim for previous weekend (?6 April).

Explained might depend on framing time. Framing needs to be beautiful. JOHN JONES of Finsbury Park are the best.

15 FEBRUARY

Another day of photography coming up. We've reviewed
the first day's shots – the proper contact sheet rather than
Polaroid's – and we've decided

– More sense of mystery needed (try a couple of ways,
  perhaps slight blurring sense of movement in the figure)
– Alice's clothing will change, all blue
– No star in the hair
– Try to make Alice's pose look unposed
– Sharpen the image of the rock pool – make it more
  obviously watery
– Like the bubbles
– Wonder if a hint of sea mist is possible to achieve (will
  steam work?)
– Think about what the side images could be if a triptych.
  Discarded the Goddess Kali effect of hands on either side
  panel

*

Seem to have moved away from incorporating any words
in the image. Still possibility of adding words to the frame.
Writing on the glass or on the cardboard boards might be too
tacky.

However, there are at least three pieces of writing that are
important here.

1. 'After Emily.'
2. 'She is…'
3. The myth.

Can we type these, print them out and add them to back
of frame?

*

SUNDAY 16 FEBRUARY

Polaroids from the shoot…

Mystery here but not enough clarity

Clearer, like the shadows on Alice's shoulder

*

Nice shadows again, like the blue

Trying to get the sea mist

Like the warm glow of this

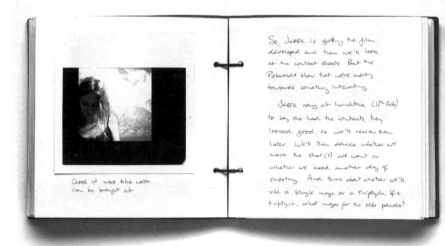

Good if more blue water can be brought out

So, Jessie is getting the film developed and then we'll look at the contact sheets. But the Polaroids show that we're moving towards something interesting.

Jessie rang at lunchtime to say she had the contacts, they looked good, so we'll review them later. We'll then decide whether we have the shot(s) we want or whether we need another day of shooting. And think about whether we'll use a single image or a triptych. If a triptych, what images for the side panels?

*

FRIDAY

The contacts were good and we chose five that we decided to get 10 x 8 prints of. A mixture of the very sharp and the very blurry – quite like both, perhaps the bigger prints will help decide.

While that's happening, Jessie finds a printer in Hackney who can do large prints by hand. Unusual to have colour shots printed by hand. Will be a bit more expensive, but there's enough in the budget and it will be worth it.

*

Anyway, the printer is in Creamer Street
        so that settles it.

This project seems full of serendipity and signs. We keep being pointed towards the next step, or see something that confirms we're going the right way.

*

[Need to find out what size hand prints we can get. Finished frame size maximum is 3m x 2m – big.

*

SATURDAY 22 FEBRUARY

I like the 10 x 8 prints. One glows beautifully – blurry deliberately.

Another is mysterious in a sharper way, and beautifully blue.

These two are my favourites. Which one? Or shall we go with both?

Perhaps both, showing our goddess Dove at different times of the day. They can be framed side by side as a diptych, or framed separately for display alongside or opposite each other.

But then I think it's just indecision to go for two, and they don't quite go together as a pair. They don't make, for example, a morning and an evening image.

So, I've chosen one that has Alice/Dove at the bottom of the frame, almost rising from the waves (if we want to keep to the memory of Botticelli's Venus). It's also the one where she looks most Botticelli-like. I think it's a lovely image, with beautiful colour – the smoke used to shoot through has enhanced the colour, giving a hint of sea mist without destroying the clarity.

*

MARCH

Various visits to the printer. The maximum size we can do is not as big as we'd hoped – to blow it up really big we'd need to have used a different camera and got a 5 x 4 negative, but we probably wouldn't have been able to achieve the effect we wanted either. So we'll have the shot as big as we can, and then have half-size shots on either side. We've chosen the three shots from the contact sheets, and there will be a dawn–noon–dusk feel to them.

*

The triptych will have something of the sun's progress across the sky to it? Let's see the final shots at their real size and then decide.

5 MARCH

The printers got the crop wrong so we have to wait till after the weekend. Annoying because I wanted to take them to the framers this weekend.

*

7 MARCH

Dominic rang and we now have dates to aim for – April 4 for delivery, April 11 for the unveiling. And the diary has to be surrendered in a couple of days, before we have the prints in the hands of the framers. Never mind.

I want each piece of writing to gain resonance from the image, and the image to gain resonance from the writing. So we have to choose the right images that interpret the writing most powerfully.

*

8 MARCH

Went to John Jones on Saturday afternoon to see about framing. Looked at options.

We've decided on three separate frames that should be mounted on the wall as triptych. The left-hand image represents the introduction/dawn, and the Dove 'She is…' poem goes with this.

*

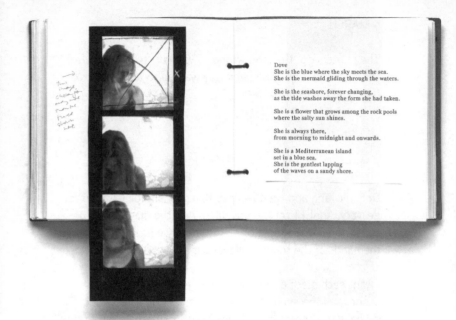

Dove
She is the blue where the sky meets the sea.
She is the mermaid gliding through the waters.

She is the seashore, forever changing,
as the tide washes away the form she had taken.

She is a flower that grows among the rock pools
where the salty sun shines.

She is always there,
from morning to midnight and onwards.

She is a Mediterranean island
set in a blue sea.
She is the gentlest lapping
of the waves on a sandy shore.

Dove

She is the blue where the sky meets the sea.
She is the mermaid gliding through the waters.

She is the seashore, forever changing,
as the tide washes away the form she had taken.
She is a flower that grows among
the rock pools where the salty sun shines.

She is always there,
from morning to midnight and onwards.

She is a Mediterranean island
set in a blue sea.
She is the gentlest lapping
of the waves on a sandy shore.

*

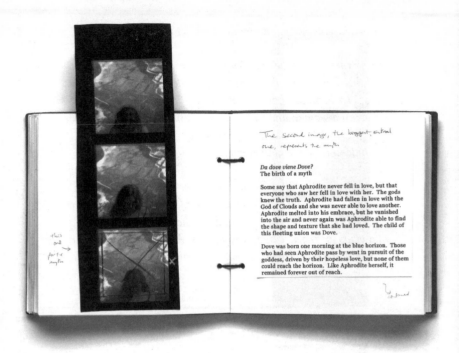

The second image, the biggest, central one, represents the
myth

Da dove viene Dove?
The birth of a myth

*Some say that Aphrodite never fell in love, but that everyone who
saw her fell in love with her. The gods knew the truth. Aphrodite
had fallen in love with the God of Clouds and she was never
able to love another. Aphrodite melted into his embrace, but he
vanished into the air and never again was Aphrodite able to find
the shape and texture that she loved. The child of this fleeting
union was Dove.*

*Dove was born one morning at the blue horizon. Those who had
seen Aphrodite pass by went in pursuit of the goddess, driven by
their hopeless love, but none of them could reach the horizon.*

Like Aphrodite herself, it remained forever out of reach.

Where the sky met the sea, Dove was born. Her bed was a rock pool, her lullaby was the lapping water, her playthings were the stars. Her birth-gift from her mother was eternal maturity; she was born a woman and she never aged after the day of the birth. The gift from her father was a blanket of sea mist, which kept her hidden from the gaze of men.

There she dwells still, never ageing, never seen, waiting for the day when her mother will rediscover her father. On that day she will be free to go her own way and find her own love. So she sits and waits for the golden dove to appear, Aphrodite's messenger that will one day bring the longed-for news.

*

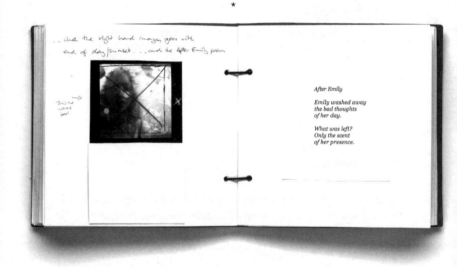

After Emily

*Emily washed away
the bad thoughts
of her day.*

*What was left?
Only the scent
of her presence.*

...and the right-hand image goes with end of day/sunset... and the 'After Emily' poem.

After Emily

Emily washed away
the bad thoughts
of her day.
What was left?
Only the scent
of her presence.

* * *

Chapter 5
Recreation and retreat

When Stuart Delves asked me, I was excited but daunted by the prospect. Would I be tutor with him on a week-long residential course at the Arvon Foundation? The course was to be called 'Creative writing for business'.

The Arvon Foundation is a wonderful not-for-profit organisation, now nearly 40 years old, that provides retreats, inspiration and development for writers. It runs courses through the year, in four rural settings, in different kinds of writing: fiction, poetry, writing for TV, film scripts, children's books, and so on. Now, for the first time, at Stuart's instigation, Arvon was interested in a business writing course, with an emphasis on creative writing. *Would I be interested in running it?* Of course I would, not least because I would learn so much myself.

Six months passed between agreeing to do it when I met Stuart at the Edinburgh Book Festival and the course happening in early Spring. During those six months we had to prepare the course and market it. It was down to Stuart and myself to recruit the 15 people we needed to make the course viable.

We managed that. The course was to be held in Totleigh Barton in Devon, near Okehampton, one week in March. I offered to collect Stuart, who was flying down from Edinburgh, at Bristol Airport and then drive us to Totleigh Barton.

* * *

Collecting Stuart from Bristol Airport in early March, I'm excited and apprehensive about the week. A week might be a long time in politics; it also seems to me a long time to be on the spot with a group of people, most of whom I don't know. Even my co-tutor Stuart is a relative unknown to me. He's a business writer based in Edinburgh who runs a writing agency called Henzteeth. We've never worked together before. We've gravitated towards each other in recent years because he likes my books and I enjoy his writing too – so we've become friendly enough, at a distance of 500 miles, to believe we can get on as co-tutors for this course. Stuart has the advantage too that ten years ago he was the director of Totleigh Barton for Arvon – he knows the place and its sometimes idiosyncratic ways.

We're reasonably well prepared, although I never feel absolutely confident of that when going into a workshop. There's always the great unknown of the people. What will they be like? Co-operators, I hope. Otherwise, why would they sign up for this course?

They have all written to us with their hopes and objectives for the course. All have slightly different slants on it but they all see the week as something of a refresher, a chance to retreat from the daily grind of work and discover (or rediscover) more of their own creativity. They might be tired with their current work, or they might even be in need of fresh enthusiasm for writing itself. They are all at different levels of their careers, some doing more writing than others. But nearly all are in the first half of their working careers; so if we can help them gain greater fulfilment in future by becoming better writers, that will be a worthwhile achievement.

* * *

We arrived at Totleigh Barton with the sun sinking on a bright, cold Monday. The house, which we reached by driving a mile down a country track, looked inviting in the late sunshine. It seemed from the number of cars that most people had already arrived. By the time Stuart and I had settled into our rooms, then wandered over to the main house, everyone was there and being briefed on the 'domestics' by the Arvon centre directors. Ian Marchant and Monique Roffey are also writers. Their role as 'centre directors' allows them to pursue their own writing in congenial surroundings; they live two miles away from Totleigh Barton.

* * *

For our first evening Ian and Monique have done the cooking. We sit there at the long refectory table eating and getting to know each other. After dinner we gather in the barn to talk. Everyone is feeling his or her way, a little apprehensive about what is to come. We ask people to say something about themselves and about their expectations for the week.

'Not sure what to expect.'
'Time and space to think.'
'Improve my confidence.'
'Not to be scared of the blank page.'
'Time away from deadlines.'
'Learn from others.'
'Freedom to experiment.'
'A new window to look out of.'
'Explore new ideas.'

We agree that writing for business should be seen as a creative activity, and it seems obvious that we've got the right group: committed but not over-anxious, interested but not desperate. Tomorrow we will start to find out more. For now we are comfortable and we spend a couple of hours in this shadowy barn, cosily heated by gas burners hanging from the ceiling, tongues loosened by glasses of wine. As midnight nears, we all retreat to our rooms. My room is like a luxurious monastic cell, the luxury provided by an electric fire, a bedside reading light and a shower. My room is in the Goosehouse, which at least sounds more promising than the five rooms located in the Pigsty.

TUESDAY

Our first morning was bright, cold and beautiful. It was my first proper look at where we were situated, in rolling Devon countryside. I walked up the hill to enjoy the surroundings and to get a mobile phone signal. As the week wore on, we all became less and less concerned about connecting with the outside world through mobile phones. Would it have been an 'infringement of civil liberties' to have banned mobile phones? There was no doubt that the absence of calls and messages helped people concentrate on their own writing.

After breakfast we gathered in the dining room that now became our writing room. I instituted the 'Quote for the day' with the following:

> 3.10 *So you will be a writer because all of a sudden you're scared of life, of its ability to sit up and bite you. You'll be a writer because books are at the same time dangerous and safe. You'll be a writer because you've done wrong and you need to do good to redeem yourself. You'll be a writer because no one will love you for what you are now and you need to compensate. You'll be a writer, not a spy, or an astronaut, or an architect.*

3.11 You are ten years old. You will be a writer. It's an accident. That's how it begins.

[James Flint, 'The accident', from Zembla *magazine)*

* * *

I should introduce you to the fifteen people on the course.

Shehnaz is Asian and no-nonsense. She claims her biggest problem is *starting*: the fear of the blank screen. For her it's definitely a screen – until she's equipped with her laptop, rather than pen and pad, she's unable to write at all. She works in public relations. By the end of the week she has less fear of blankness, more confidence in her ability.

Andrew works in Copenhagen for a Danish multinational that decided two years ago that English was going to be the company's everyday language of business. He's worked there for eight years, having married a Danish woman. He wants to re-establish a stronger connection with his own creativity and his native language.

Laura works for a London brand consultancy in naming and writing. She studied sciences at Cambridge and has gradually come to realise that she is by inclination more of an artist. So she wants to go away from here feeling that she is a real writer.

Kevin is an IT consultant in his mid-fifties, now setting up his own business. Through that business he sees himself as an IT translator, making sense of technology for those (like me) who don't understand it.

Michal is Australian and works for Unilever. She has an air of confidence that comes from her country and her company. As customer innovation manager she spends a lot of time motivating people to change. So she needs persuasive words.

Kathryn comes from the same Edinburgh PR company as Shehnaz. Lively, with a lovely Scottish accent, she claims a lack of confidence in her writing ability, a desire to open her mind to fresh angles.

Kath is also from Unilever where she is part of the team running the Catalyst programme on arts and creativity. Her background is in the visual arts. Her role at work is finding ways to inspire people through the arts, making the arts relevant to working life. So she has to sell, and she wants to find out how to sell better.

Jayne is a writer with a Yorkshire-based design and identity company. She hopes the week will be something of a retreat from the constant tyranny of deadlines, a time to reflect and experiment.

Will is from a company that specialises in the design of websites and printed communications for the public and not-for-profit sectors. He's just joined in the last month, having been recruited from the ICA, so it's quite a remarkable sign of faith that his own company has sent him straight off to this week.

Olivia is from the same company as Will and the reason why Will was sent here. It's a good sign of Olivia's management skills. She works as a strategist and project manager, with responsibilities for getting new business. So she wants proof of writing's potential to convince her clients.

Hanlie works in internal communications at BP. Originally from South Africa, she deals with people from all around the world to write and edit case studies of their work. She wants to put more creativity into her writing.

Damian is a graphic designer, born in Northern Ireland, now living and working in Scotland. He has worked with Stuart, so he believes in the creative power of words in business. He now wants to learn more so that he can apply it to the new company he is forming.

Caroline is from a Nottingham design and writing agency that works a lot with Boots. She sees the benefits of writing well for clients, now she wants to feel it more, develop skills and convince clients in the argument.

Kay is a writer at the same agency as Caroline. She wants to expand her creative writing skills and explore new ideas that she can then apply to business clients.

Tim is an independent writer who was a design journalist before moving into more corporate areas of writing, like annual reports. He's looking for freedom to experiment – and fresh air in a literal and metaphorical sense.

* * *

We learnt more about people from the first exercise, which was based on favourite books. Choices ranged from Hans Christian Andersen to *The Wasp Factory*, from Seamus Heaney's *Beowulf* to John Irving's *A Prayer for Owen Meaney*. Everyone was articulate about their books, keen to evangelise about books that meant a lot to them.

The first exercise was an enjoyable way of getting into the day's theme of 'putting yourself into your language'. We did this more directly through the next exercise that was about producing an autobiographical piece of writing about their lives so far. Starting with some interesting titles – 'So…', 'One part of me', 'Positively cynical' – people wrote the opening paragraph of their autobiographies, as in this example by Kath.

'You'll enjoy it once you get there.'
She's always right, my mum. Well, there was the incident with
the lemon meringue pie, but I think we can all agree that's best
forgotten. So when she tells me I'll enjoy it once I get there, my
arguments are really only half-hearted, whether 'it' is a ballet
class, a Brownie pack holiday, a new job in a foreign country
or an ex-boyfriend's wedding. She reminds me that I was born
two and a half weeks late, quite comfortable where I was thank
you very much, no burning urge to see new places and meet new
people. And that turned out alright. So I go along to the whatever,
wherever, and I do enjoy it. Apart from the ex-boyfriend's
wedding, that was a disaster, but we'll get to that later.'

We followed this with an exercise inspired by Roger
McGough's poem 'In Two Minds'. The idea is to create a circular
thought process about loves and hates. There is always a
positive side to the negative, and vice versa. I particularly liked
this one by Kevin.

What I love about sound
*   is the absence of silence*
What I hate about silence
*   is its hollow emptiness*
What I love about emptiness
*   is that it's like a well going down forever*
What I hate about forever
*   is that it never ends*
What I love about ends
*   is that they're not starts*
What I hate about starts
*   is that sense of beginning*
What I love about beginning
*   is the first chord of its opening sound*
What I hate about sound
*   is the absence of silence.*

The morning passed quickly with these and other exercises. They were up and running, initial doubts about 'Can I?/Dare I?' fell away, encouraged by the fact that everyone was taking risks. It's not easy to put your own personality into your writing and then expose it to the hearing of people who yesterday were strangers. But once they had done, you could feel the liberation.

In the afternoon we sent people out into the countryside, gathering sights and objects that became the starting points for pieces of automatic writing. After this Stuart introduced the idea to the group that everyone should work on a personal piece, in addition to all the other exercises. This piece – poem, prose, fact or fiction – would be needed for the final evening.

Cooking was done on a rota basis. A group of four went off to prepare the evening meal. By the time we gathered in the barn after dinner that evening it was clear that the group had bonded. Two haikus the next day, by Will, showed how the cooking feeds into the creative process.

Haiku # 1: The Division of Labour
Mashing is my job.
I leave the fish to others
And also the sauce.

Haiku # 2: Pasta Dish Blues
The dishwasher whirrs.
Two minutes and all is done.
Except, cheese remains.

In the evening Stuart and I provided the entertainment by reading from our own work, business and personal. I read a couple of 'mirror poems' as I have called them. The idea is to take an older poem, from the fifteenth or sixteenth centuries, and 'translate' it into a modern form. I had taken four poems, all personal favourites – by Wyatt, Donne, Herbert, Sidney – and written my own version, keeping to the same poetic form as the original, but putting the language and the thinking into more contemporary terms. My thought was not 'these old poets need a bit of help to make them relevant' – far from it. As a writer I found the process of 'translation' a powerful way to add depth to my reading of the originals. I saw this as an exercise that aided both reading and writing. The constraints of the particular poetic form were a challenge that developed comprehension and skills. So I suggested this exercise of rewriting – not necessarily of poetry – as a useful way to hone writing ability.

Here are two examples, showing the original and my 'translated' version.

Just Exchange

My true love hath my heart and I have his,
By just exchange one for another given:
I holde his deare, and mine he cannot misse,
There never was a better bargaine driven.
My true love hath my heart and I have his.
My heart in me keepes him and me in one,
My heart in him his thoughts and senses guides:
He loves my heart, for once it was his owne,
I cherish him because in me it bides.
My true love hath my heart and I have his.
   [Sir Philip Sidney, 1554–1596]

Fair Deal
I love him and he loves me, heart and soul.
The deal is fair for I am his, he mine.
Never was one so dear, so cheaply sold,
No better bargain of the two for one kind.
I love him and he loves me, heart and soul.
My love and his are both within my heart,
My every thought is shared inside his mind.
Like twins our love cannot be put apart,
We are both bound, but never feel the bind.
I love him and he loves me, heart and soul.
   [2004]

Death be not proud, though some have called thee
Mighty and dreadfull, thou art not soe,
For, those, whom thou think'st, thou dost overthrow,
Die not, poore death, nor yet canst thou kill mee.
From rest and sleepe, which but thy pictures bee,
Much pleasure, then from thee, much more must flow,
And soonest our best men with thee doe goe,
Rest of their bones and soules deliverie.
Thou art slave to Fate, Chance, Kings, and desperate men,
And dost with poison, warre and sicknesse dwell,
And poppie, or charmes can make us sleepe as well,
And better than thy stroake; why swell'st thou then?
One short sleepe past, wee wake eternally,
And death shall be no more; death thou shalt die.

   [John Donne, 1572–1631]

I scorn you, Death, you're no big deal; though some
Go cold when whispering your name, I don't;
Although you think you'll murder me, you won't,
Your power is weak, your strength soon overcome.
We love to sleep, make living bodies numb,
Imitate your certain meeting, though we can't
Yet taste the joy of greeting you, we shan't
Delay too long, release is sure to come.
The truth is this: you sail a sorry ship
A crew of all that's bad. You have no hope.
We find oblivion through drink or dope,
No need for you: why think we're in your grip?
We'll sleep, we'll wake, it will be everlasting
And Death, you will be gone, a bell that's passing.

   [2004]

The Totleigh Barton barn on a cold evening, with the gas burners and red wine glowing, was a comfortable setting. Stuart read from his own work, poetry and prose. The wine slipped down easily, taking the work with it, and we all had vivid dreams that night.

* * *

WEDNESDAY

Another beautiful morning, bright and frosty. I start with a walk up the hill to get mobile phone reception and check if I have messages. The world continues to revolve outside Totleigh Barton, but it's satisfying to make it wait by walking back down to the house. People gather for breakfast. Damian makes porridge – *no thanks*. Aside from the evening meal, the eating arrangements are very informal. Just help yourself.

* * *

Time to start with another Quote of the Day.

Summer 1995. I was at an artist's colony in the woods. For weeks I had been trying to write about the burning of Smyrna in 1922 and was getting nowhere. Stupidly I thought I could manage the thing by imagination alone. Rather than doing research, I sat down at my desk day after day and tried to summon up a bygone Asia Minor from what little I knew or could make up. One day I fell into despair. I was ready to give up the novel. I left the studio and wandered the mansion. As I came up the formal staircase, I passed the reading table where the colony keeps literary magazines and books by former guests. My eye alighted on a book. It was a historical account called Smyrna 1922.

I had come across this description by Jeffrey Eugenides in the *Guardian*. He had gone on to write *Middlesex* and there is a particularly vivid section of writing about the burning of Smyrna in 1922. I believe in that kind of coincidence. Sometimes your writing can be driven in a certain direction by a chance event. When writing the Guinness stories I had not known how to conclude them. Wandering around Dublin one afternoon I came upon Trinity College and saw a poster for an exhibition. This exhibition of the *Book of Kells* was called 'Turning darkness into light'. Two weeks earlier Guinness had launched new TV advertising with the end line 'Out of darkness comes light'. Suddenly, almost with a blinding sense of epiphany, I had a location and character for the final chapter of my story.

The quotation also related to a reading I had given the previous day from *Mnemonic* by the Theatre de Complicité. The point of that reading was to show the close connection between imagination and memory. Sometimes we are too mystical about imagination. We almost apostrophise it like the romantic poets, calling upon the Muse to help our writing. Imagination can be more mundane than that; it need not descend upon us from the ether. As Jeffrey Eugenides found, you can try to force it too hard. Often we can lubricate it by the power of research or memory.

* * *

The Wednesday morning exercises explored this theme of drawing on experiences. We started with writing about 'What was the first proper day of your career?' – a question deliberately ambiguous. Then we talked about examples that people had brought with them of both good and bad writing for business. This helps to establish a discipline of reading written work critically in the world around us. There was no shortage of bad examples, some of them very funny, but the good examples were thinner on the ground. Innocent Drinks was cited several times, along with examples from Sony, Howie's, First Direct and Lonely Planet.

From here we did work on finding a theme, introduced by Stuart with a brief he had been given. Then, through a series of exercises, we went on a treasure trail to find out more about individual words. I had brought a large part of my own reference library – I added this to the Totleigh Barton collection and then encouraged people to follow the trail of a single word. After this we wrote myths about the gods or goddesses of particular words or concepts. This exercise, as ever, produced fresh insights into some of the most hackneyed words in the business world.

After lunch Stuart and I held the first of our surgeries for individuals. We saw six people for half an hour each, to talk about any particular writing concerns and to give guidance on what to develop when they returned to work the following week. This set the pattern for the afternoons on the next two days, with surgeries for each individual. For those not involved in the surgeries it was a time to work on personal pieces or on the project we had set at the end of the morning.

The starting point was a favourite word. From this word individuals developed initial ideas for a new brand, product or company. Then we put people in pairs because collaborative working is a necessary skill for business writers to develop. Perhaps that is the biggest difference from the work of a purely literary writer. The poet or novelist writes entirely as an individual. The business writer cannot avoid the need to work with others, whether as partners, team members, briefers, creative developers, critics, editors or clients. It is similar to the difference between a designer and fine artist. But as the designer can be, indeed should be, inspired by the fine artist, so too the business writer should be inspired by the literary writer.

* * *

The poet Jackie Wills arrived in the late afternoon. Having worked with Jackie and admired her poetry, I had invited her to Devon to give a reading in the evening. So, after dinner, we all gathered in the barn, and Jackie read from her collections, including her latest, *Fever Tree*. Hearing a poet read her own poems adds depth to the experience. It shines a different light on your understanding of poetry, and it means that you always hear that poet's voice when you return later to the poems. As reading your writing out loud had become an important theme of the week, it reinforced the value of performing and listening to writing.

When Jackie and I had worked together at Lever Fabergé, a number of redundancies had been made in that team because of the market conditions. It had meant that we were working with an anxious and slightly demotivated group for a period. Jackie and I had discussed the situation. I was more familiar with it than she was, having been through similar scenarios in companies where I had worked previously. Jackie responded in a personal and human way to it, in the way she knew best.

She wrote a poem called 'Recession' that came out of our discussions.

Recession
for John Simmons

An express rips through our daily papers
and those of us foolishly standing
beyond the yellow line on platform 13
at Clapham Junction are dragged in its wake

towards Gatwick airport. Flapping around
in the turbulence, I overhear a man
in his early fifties tell a young woman
he's just been made redundant.

I strain to hear more. 'Two or three days,'
he says. She mutters a response, too quiet,
but I catch 'agency'. As he talks he's pulling
his trousers up at the back. 'It could be worse.'

He throws that line away. It tumbles
onto the platform at Horley. I yell, 'What now?'
but an express passing the other way scoops
the two of them up, back towards London.

When I arrive at work, the news I shouldn't know
but do, has nowhere to go. Two guys, half-joking,
plan a wake. I hear each word. Every office
should have a noise machine, programmed

to send out random bursts of pneumatic drill,
to offset the building's shock-absorbent hush,
which is interrupted only by phones,
the occasional thud of another job hitting the floor.

Jackie read for about an hour, while we all became her audience. It was engrossing, sitting back to absorb words that had a mesmeric power in the poet's personal reading. I looked around and could see people gripped by a new understanding. The subsequent informal discussion proved that. I sensed we now had more than one poet in our company, and I started to feel excited about the writing that our group would produce at the end of the week for their personal pieces.

THURSDAY

Jackie had left by the time we all got up next morning, whisked off by a taxi to the station so that she could return to her family in Brighton. At breakfast people were still buzzing with the idea of poetry. That morning's Quote of the Day was relevant.

I liked the poems long before I understood them.
[James Fenton]

Understanding the meaning of that quotation was a breakthrough for many people in the group. Three days had made a big difference.

* * *

That morning we worked on 'tone of voice'. In the modern business world, where the brand is such a central concept, tone of voice becomes ever more important. Brand managers increasingly accept the truth that brands communicate through their language, perhaps even more than through the visual language of logos, colours and graphics that we have traditionally recognised them by.

We worked on a series of exercises, drawing on poetic and storytelling techniques. We used newspapers too as easy exemplars of tone of voice – it's clear that the language of the *Sun* is different from the *Guardian* and the *Daily Mail*.

We discovered too the value of writing within constraints, the liberation that can come from adhering to specific disciplines. The exercises on metaphors and creating characters by responding to questions made this our most intense and rewarding session. We knew that everyone was now completely engaged, and the afternoon surgeries confirmed this. While we ran the surgeries, people worked in their pairs on the project to develop a brand.

* * *

That evening in the barn Stuart and I read from some of our favourite writers. Stuart reinforced the previous evening's relaxation into poetry by reading from Bernard O'Donoghue and John Burnside. My main reading was from John Irving's *The World according to Garp*: there is a wonderful section where Garp is inventing a story for his son, raising questions about reality and imagination, truth and storytelling.

As we all talked afterwards people remarked how much they enjoyed the experience of listening and being read to. There was something comfortingly nostalgic in it, taking everyone back to memories of childhood. And a realisation that, back in the daily routine of daytime working followed by evening recovery from working, we have lost an important and easily accessible pleasure. The availability of modern entertainment has dulled our appetite for the most natural of entertainments – that of reading and storytelling.

FRIDAY

The last day dawned, but for the first time that week it was cloudy. Rain was coming. I enjoyed the morning walk up the hill and after breakfast read the final Quote of the Day.

Because to write is to feel your way step by step along a thread of beauty. Along the thread of a poem, or of a story unfolding on a sheet of silk. For the poet, like the tightrope walker, must go forward, word by word, page by page, along the path of a book. And the most difficult thing is not that you must keep your footing on the rope of language, with only a pen for balance; not to keep going straight ahead, when the way is blocked by the sudden drop of a comma, or the obstacle of a full stop. No, the difficulty for the poet is to stay on the rope that is writing, to live every moment without losing sight of his dream, and to never come down, not even for a second, from the rope of the imagination.

[Snow, Maxence Fermine]

* * *

Friday morning was our most raucous session. I think we planned it that way but by this stage everything was progressing with its own momentum. Seven teams had been working on seven new brands that they had created. They each presented these to all of us, amid much laughter and mutual support. Uncannily a couple of the brand ideas were similar in their essence, but quite different in the ways that they had then been developed. We were presented with brand descriptions, advertising campaigns, press releases, chairman's talks. All were amazingly credible. Not entirely frivolously we suggested that the brands should be registered legally.

After the presentations, we came down to practicalities again with jargon-busting editing advice. By this point the work on business writing was done; people's energies were already turning towards the personal pieces that they would finish writing that afternoon to read in the barn that evening.

* * *

The afternoon passed with surgeries with myself and Stuart. People came to us for half-hour sessions, then returned to their writing or, if that was the way the rota worked out, to preparing the evening meal. There was a feeling of anticipation: everyone was excited, if a little apprehensive, at the prospect of reading their work in public. The more personal writing becomes, the more difficult it is to expose to public scrutiny. But writers know that they have to put themselves through this delicious agony.

There is a particular resonance to the last supper. Even without the Biblical reference, sharing a meal can have a memorable impact. It is a ritual deep in our psyche. There is a mixture of looking back and looking forward, sadness and joy in the changing cycle. This was the last time this group of fifteen, plus Stuart and myself, would meet in this way. We were aware that, in this week, we had shared an experience that would remain with us. At the heart of that experience was a shared love of words and writing.

We gathered in the barn after dinner. This evening we had to scuttle from our rooms to the barn through driving rain. As we sat inside, we could hear rain on the roof. There was a darkness outside thicker than the majority of us city-dwellers were used to. I remembered *Beowulf* that Damian had brought as a favourite book. It was time for a drink in the mead hall.

Ian Marchant sat in on our session that evening, drawn by the excitement he had discovered in talking to people through the day. We all sat around in a circle, then I invited someone to go first. Obviously nervous, and keen to get the trial out of the way, Hanlie volunteered. She read two poems, having not written a poem since school days. She did well; the poems were good; we were under way.

After that there was less reluctance. People simply stepped forward and read their pieces. There were poems, travel writing, short stories inspired by exercises we had done earlier that week; a couple of autobiographical extracts that were funny and vigorous; more poetry. Some of the pieces were long, although no one exceeded the limit of ten minutes. The standard was uniformly high; everyone produced work to be proud of. Here is a selection:

Take up your fingers

take up your fingers and press them to the walls,
kissing the cool whiteness with each pink tip
as you trace the perfect imperfections,
print to print with yesterdays

find your knife and sink it into the flesh
plunge it deep and pull down
watch the plaster peel back and the brick-dust flesh
spill moments of its memory on the floor

listen hard and you'll hear them
as they sigh free their secrets, start their stories,
let the words whispered within them so long
fall out and fill up the room where you stand

mind your step as they swirl round your legs
screams streaming into your ears and tears
puddling on the floor while laughter licks your feet
and love poems at last find room to romance
   [Caroline Triptree]

Without words

As the sun slides heavy down on distant fields, the broiling white rage of the day burnt to a sullen pink, we listen. We listen to the fug of dusk mosquitos whining their hungry drone. We listen to the voice inside.

It's day six of our seven-day retreat in Bodhgaya, our second in silence. We listen because we cannot speak.

There are fifteen of us residents at The Root Institute, a small cluster of whitewashed buildings ranged around a sunscorched lawn on the outskirts of the small, dusty, north-eastern Indian town of Bodhgaya. It's one of many Buddhist meditation centres in Bodhgaya, literally translated the town of the Bodhi. It's here, under a Bodhi tree, that Siddartha reached enlightenment. It's here that Buddhism was born.

Like Siddartha before us, we've come in search of enlightenment. Or, at least, a clean bed and some peace and quiet for the week. We're travellers from around the globe, shabby from Indian train journeys, cheap guesthouses and endless bartering, drawn, all of us, by the promise of candlelit stupas, flower-strewn Buddhas and temples of incense, ritual, and almost certain epiphany. Like many before us, we've made the pilgrimage, like many before us, we're not sure why, like many before us, we've come to find out.

The course starts with Buddhist teachings, explained over long mornings and afternoons cross-legged in a bare-stone room called the gompa. They are followed by meditations on big ideas like impermanence, non-attachment, the ego and death. We grapple with the questions. We wonder where we end and the universe starts, we wonder who we are and why we're here, we wonder if we've done the right thing, if we'll make the week.

*Next it's silence. Can you imagine? A day, or two, or three,
without words. Try it. Silence. It brings a new meaning to words.
For the second half of our week, we're asked not to speak, and,
if we can, not to write or read. A holiday from words? Or a
sentence to silence? We wonder how it will feel. How will we
cope with silence? How will we cope without words?*

*Our holiday from words was everything a good holiday should
be, relaxed, refreshing, easy. Being free of words highlighted the
good about language. How words capture our thoughts, express
our ideas, shape our experience, how they make us friends, paint
us pictures, inspire belief. It also highlighted the bad. How we
abuse words as well as use them, how they allow us to be lazy as
well as vital, how they make excuses for what we're not willing
to do, how they conspire with us to be dishonest, how they limit
as well as liberate our perceptions. It's funny what silence does to
you. I'm not sure I want to speak just yet.*

   [Jayne Workman]

Searching

My words are lost.
I've sent out a search party.
They're looking everywhere.
They started as you'd expect,
Scanning the fields as if
They're paid for each square metre covered by nightfall.
But they're narrowing it down.
They're becoming stealthily sly.
They're looking in the prints of city shoes on mud,
Setting birdsong to play on repeat.
They told me to wait here
In case one found its own way home.
So I'm staying by my window, anxious, at my desk.
The small part of thatch I can see
Looks like a thousand dead fingerbones,
All pointing the way.
   [Laura Forman]

Extracts from 'A Phrase Book for the High Weald
of Sussex'

Local greetings

*If you have arranged to meet someone somewhere, like a public
house, you may be greeted by phrases such as:*

'Good grief, how totally unexpected to see you here.'

Or:

'Why are you hanging around here like a pervert?'
These are both signs of friendship, and may lead to...

Pub chat

*The friendly and generous folk of the Weald will be delighted to
engage you in conversation. They may invite you into a smoky
snug, or simply back you into a tight spot between the roaring
log fire and the bar. Phrases you may hear:*

'Would it be most inconvenient if I was to request a modest
replenishment?'

Translation: Would you buy me a drink?

'I believe the landlord has both hands free.'

Translation: Would you buy me a drink?

'There is a scandalous amount of light shining through
my glass.'

Translation: Would you buy me a drink?

Chat may also include:
'Might you be kind enough to furnish me with a snout?'
Don't be alarmed, they are not asking for facial surgery. This
is simply a request for a cigarette, preferably a Rothmans, or a
Winston if that's all you happen to have about your person. You
can assume that a light will also be required, and may prefer
to simply 'write-off' your box of matches rather than spend all
evening wondering whether it will be returned. Keep Zippo
lighters out of sight.

A further note on safety and security

At points throughout the evening small, wiry men may appear
in the pub with, say, a brace of pheasants or a dead badger
hidden inside their coat. Do not agree to buy these, even if they
allow you to stroke them first, or suggest they can be made into
a coat.

If the locals seem particularly jolly you may hear them say:
'We've been in conversation with Mary Jane.' This means they
have been smoking marijuana (it's not called the High Weald
for nothing). Be careful, they may corner you and start to discuss
ley lines, UFOs or classic Wealden bands such as Tolkien
Heads, or Jack the Spliffer.

Caution is also advised if you are taken into a particularly loud
section of a pub and introduced to the local drug dealer. You
may find that the £20 you hand over buys a collection of small
baskets for use in the garden.

Greetings for unexpected meetings

While you may find High Wealden folk reserved during the
day, they can be most gregarious and free of spirit in the
evening. A native welcome is always to be had, and on

*wandering into a hostelry and bumping into an acquaintance
you may hear:*

'Good Lord, I haven't seen you for about 3 million years.'

Or even:

'My word, if it isn't Mr. Timothy Rich.'
    [Tim Rich]

    With the readings completed, a great deal of mutual
congratulation followed. The group supported itself; everyone
was pleased that they had all made a transition to become,
more confidently and more certainly, writers. The suggestion
that Stuart and I had made a couple of days ago was now
adopted as the necessary endorsement of the week. Everyone
would submit their best pieces and we would publish them
as *The E-Thing*, an electronic version of a book that we
would email to everyone. Damian volunteered to design it.
At everyone's request, Stuart agreed to include his response
to one of my metaphor exercises. In this everyone had fixed
on a person they knew well, then produced a series of lines
prompted by my suggestions of themes – what place, what time
of day, what colour do you associate with this person?

The Poet

He is a battered old Escort,
with straw trailing from the crumpled boot.
He is snowy white,
flecked with the feathers of grey doves.
He is a swathe of reeds down by the bog lands
in the field he gazes over.
He is a tramp's overcoat,
pockets stuffed with pored-over Guardians.
He is the crags of the Cuillins
where the snows don't leave till May,
where the winds whine like ghosts.
He is a large dram of Talisker,
sherried with the sing-song of his voice.
He is the early morning sun
hitting his shades
as he walks to the bus hut for his newspaper.
He is the sound of water, rolling over stones,
outside the window where he sleeps.

   [Stuart Delves]

SATURDAY

Up early, showering, dressing, packing, then carrying my belongings of the week across the courtyard to my car. At six o'clock in early March it was still dark. Stuart and Damian had a plane to catch at Bristol Airport and I needed to drive them there.

We were not an exuberant trio as we drove along with sun rising over Dartmoor. Perhaps it was the Leonard Cohen music I had chosen to play, moody and atmospheric but encouraging reflection. Perhaps it was the early hour; I am not made for conversation at breakfast time, particularly when I have had no breakfast. But more likely it was the impact of the week, satisfaction mingled with sadness that it had come to an end; and the realisation that it would be good to be home but that home was still many hours driving away.

By the end of the week we had a group of fifteen people who now considered themselves as real writers. Not only had they produced poetry, stories and many other kinds of creative writing, they would continue to do so. Writing was now part of them, it had shaped their perception of themselves, it had formed their new identity. They had made a decision to ensure that creative writing was embedded in their personal and business lives. They had made the link too between the creativity they had found inside themselves and the creativity they could put into their work. The two areas of writing were not separate. In fact, each supported the other. It was an enormous gain, this revelation they had seen, this knowledge they had gained from experience. They had become dark angels.

Chapter 6
Writing right

It might seem strange, particularly after the diary extracts in the last two chapters, but keeping a diary is something I don't do. Perhaps now I need to reconsider. I do carry around a notebook, but I have never made an attempt to keep notes and thoughts as a *daily* discipline.

However, having written about writing short and writing long, I decided that this chapter needed to be about writing right. An impossible aspiration perhaps. Who knows what is right? Leafing through my notebook I came across these words spoken by the Arsenal footballer Thierry Henry, probably the best player in the world as I write this book.

Perfection doesn't exist, but the quest for it makes you better.

So, in the footsteps of Thierry Henry, let's go on a quest in this chapter to try to make ourselves better writers. As with football, training is important; but training for a writer will almost inevitably involve more solitary activities than for a player of team sports. Writing workshops help to bring writers together and to learn from each other by doing the same exercises. But you cannot have a daily diet of workshops: you need to practise and develop your writing in a disciplined way.

One discipline I have maintained for more than 20 years is my practice of writing on a Friday evening. I finish 'work' then get down to serious writing by 8 o'clock on Friday evening. I have a study, I shut myself away, the phone never rings about work on a Friday evening. After 20 years I have stopped thinking of it as strange; it's simply what I do. Most of this book, for example, has been written on a succession of Friday evenings.

So, in thinking about writing right, I decided it was time – for one week at least – to change my discipline a little. To move from notebook to diary. To keep a daily record from one Friday evening to the next Friday evening, and simply see what turns up that illuminates the subject of our quest. Writing in the spirit of Dickens' Mr Micawber...

'My dear Copperfield,' said Mr Micawber, putting out his hand, 'this is indeed a meeting which is calculated to impress the mind with a sense of the instability and uncertainty of all humans – in short, it is a most extraordinary meeting. Walking along the street, reflecting upon the probability of something turning up (of which I am at present rather sanguine) I find a young but valued friend turn up, who is connected with the most eventful period of my life; I may say, with the turning-point of my existence. Copperfield, my dear fellow, how do you do?'

If we want to improve as writers, we have to learn from great authors. To improve your business writing, I point you towards novelists and poets rather than business texts. If you have stayed with me this far into the book, I believe that you must share my faith in the power of great writing. Charles Dickens might not be the man you can call on to write your next business plan, but there is still much he can teach us about the sheer vitality of language used with pleasure. A hundred and fifty years on and Dickens' language is not that of the twenty-first century street, but it still crackles with energy and invention. Don't we all want to write with energy and invention? How can we take inspiration from Dickens and apply that to our business writing? More than any other writer, Dickens has inspired me to want to write, but he has never made me want to imitate him. He is, after all, 'the great inimitable'. In workshops, my favourite exercise still revolves around people talking and writing about their favourite book. Sometimes the reaction has surprised me – participants contact me afterwards to thank me for reminding them to read again. Think about books that live in your memory. Why do they mean so much to you? What makes the emotional connection between you and that book? What is it that still holds your gaze like the Ancient Mariner or walks purposefully up to you and says 'How do you do?' like an old friend.

* * *

FRIDAY 14 MAY

A draining day. A day that ends at my desk, writing under the anglepoise light, with David Byrne singing in the background. A very public day, having to give a performance. Today I gave a two-hour event for the marketing department of Kimberly-Clark in Reigate. A lively group representing brands like Kleenex, Huggies and Kotex. The event was a combination of scripted talk and workshop. To give more theatre to the performance, I was helped by my colleagues Neil Taylor and Julie Batty who read and acted parts of the script. In between the audience examined Kimberly-Clark's own tone of voice, looking at ways to improve their words in external and internal communication. My theme, at their request, was 'Clarity'. Clarity is always the easiest way for a business to approach the subject of writing. It seems to be something that no one in a company can possibly argue with. 'Of course we all want to be clear'.

They might have thought me perverse then to argue at times against clarity. Only because I want to raise the emotional content of writing at work. The more emotional your writing, the more possibilities for misunderstanding. But writing that simply aims for clarity, and nothing but clarity, squeezing out any trace of ambiguity and playfulness from language, ends up losing its purpose. Writing that is clear but cold, dry and entirely objective can fail because we find it boring. We simply don't read it; our brains disengage from it. You cannot be clear if you are not read.

A highlight – at least for me – was Julie reading out the last page of James Joyce's *Ulysses*. Following the astounding success of Lynne Truss's *Eats, Shoots and Leaves: The Zero Tolerance Approach to Punctuation*, I wanted to establish that great writing can break the rules of pedantry. But first you have to know what the rules are.

* * *

I will use extracts from some favourite books during the rest of this chapter. Start by going to the last few pages of *Ulysses*. Don't worry that you will spoil the book by reading the end first – it is not that kind of book. But not all my favourite writing is fiction. In keeping with the 'diary' theme, here is an extract from Simon Hoggart's *Playing to the Gallery*. Simon Hoggart is the funniest and most consistent of political diarists, his observations of people are sharp but never cruel. There is an almost affectionate strain in his satire. Here he writes about the linguistic peculiarities of the British Deputy Prime Minister, John Prescott.

> *You have to think of the speech itself as a chap who is taking his large, bouncy dog – a Great Prescott perhaps – for a walk in the country. Prescott is on a lead, of course, because there are sheep in the fields. But he can't just stroll along. He tugs and pulls at the speech, trying to force it to go the way he wants. Some of these tugs are just small twitches: 'That is something we are particularly, and proud of'.*

It's easy to laugh at John Prescott because he has his own strange way with words. They just seem to come out of his mouth in a fairly random pattern but actually he's far more intelligible when you simply listen to him rather than read him. Many politicians are like that, especially since the television soundbite has replaced the debating speech as the measure of political success. There was a very funny book that collected the press statements of Donald Rumsfeld, chopped them up into lines that looked like verse, and published them as *Pieces of Intelligence: The Existential Poetry of Donald H. Rumsfeld*. Here's one of the poems.

The Unknown

As we know,
There are known knowns.
There are things we know we know.
We also know
There are known unknowns.
That is to say
We know there are some things
We do not know.
But there are also unknown unknowns,
The ones we don't know we don't know.

[12 February 2002, Department of Defense news briefing]

John Prescott and Donald Rumsfeld are warnings to me of the danger of a principle that I advocate – 'write as if you were speaking'. The fact is we all speak without paying too much attention to the most basic rules of grammar, such as the need to end sentences before going onto new ones. So if I advise 'write as if you were speaking', I would also emphasise the need to 'edit, edit, edit'. When you are writing you have more opportunities to edit than when you are speaking.

So my conclusions at the end of my first diary evening are that conviction, self-belief, sheer force of personality are essential qualities you need to put into your writing. The business world – corporate writing – tries to suppress those qualities in its writers. If we allow that suppression to take place we allow corporate-speak to triumph. That's why we need to side with the dark angels.

* * *

SATURDAY 15TH MAY

Today it's the headline that makes the headline. The *Daily Mirror* front page says 'SORRY… WE WERE HOAXED'. All the other papers have this as a main story, and the broadcast media have also been full of the sacking of the *Daily Mirror* editor for publishing faked pictures of British soldiers maltreating Iraqi prisoners. So the tabloid editor departs for relying too heavily on pictures and failing to say the words that appeared as today's headline. We still live in societies where words matter.

In the UK, the Chairman and Director General of the BBC have departed over a few contentious words. In the US the President and senior members of the government squirm under questioning, revealing greater discomfort with the deployment of language than with the deployment of weapons. If heroes fall, they are often brought low by words.

But it's Saturday, a big football day and relief from whatever else is happening in the world. This afternoon, at Highbury for a couple of hours, I had only to think about and enjoy Arsenal's latest and greatest triumph – winning the Premiership and finishing the season unbeaten. Here is a team with an idolised captain who is French, born in Senegal and a speaker of eloquent English. The increasingly cosmopolitan nature of top football has brought about enormous changes in my lifetime. The mixture of nationalities that is now commonplace in football would have been unimaginable when I first started watching in the 1950s. And English has evolved to reflect this cultural mix.

* * *

Last year I was in the US to give a couple of talks about language, to promote *The Invisible Grail*. One was in New York, the other in Baltimore. For the Baltimore talk – attended by people from advertising and marketing agencies and their clients, and held in the 'Versailles Room' of a central hotel – I asked people to write down examples of words in every day use in American English that had originated in non-English languages. My point, my hope, was to demonstrate that we all understand 'fusion English', a version of language that draws on recent borrowings from all around the world.

Having gathered the examples in, I promised to email the words back to the group as a 'story'. Not surprisingly, words with a food association dominated. Here is the story I produced.

Versailles in Baltimore, chandeliers and damask. After, the restaurant, haute cuisine with a salsa twist. Bistro or bodega? Smorgasbord or tapas? Hors d'oeuvres or burritos? Dim sum or goulash? All prêt a manger.

'What's the quid pro quo?'
'Nada. Zip. Zilch.'
'Yo, you loco?'
'Aloha.'
'Siesta or fiesta, hombre?'
'A coffee in the café. Cappucino, café au lait, latte.'
'Kindergarten stuff.'

Chic in his chinos, he had je ne sais quoi, an esprit de corps, a savoir faire.

'Try a haiku, samurai.'
'You mean wasabi?'
'It's de rigueur.'
'I prefer dolcelatte.'

I guess it's the zeitgeist. Tête à tête with tamales, schadenfreude sets in, the bidet beckons. Passé perhaps, like yesterday's baguettes. Manana manana, et cetera et cetera.

'Adios, amigo.'
'Ciao.'

Capisce? Gracias.

The only point is to say that language is fun. As writers in English let's enjoy the constant trade in words that is happening daily. And try it for yourself – keep an ear open for new words entering the language from other languages. Perhaps they come as asylum seekers, perhaps as guests of honour. Whatever way we should make them welcome, as other languages give shelter to our travelling words.

* * *

SUNDAY 16TH MAY

A family day, with nine of us for Sunday lunch. The family gathering revolves around my father-in-law, Jim, an ex-docker now in his eighties, having survived two heart by-pass operations. He's a natural storyteller. When Jessie my daughter went away for a year, the thing she missed most was Granddad's stories. These are personal tales of East End life in London, what it was like to live in the 1930s through to the 1960s, where his memories are strongest and the storytelling most vivid.

He marks a clear demarcation line between generations, yet the younger generations want to include him in their lives. Today he returns to a familiar theme, his personal hatred of the word 'kids' to describe children. 'They're not the offspring of a goat', he splutters in his rant.

The best of his stories today was about Birdy the butcher; a lifelong bachelor. Why did he never marry? It seemed women customers would go into his butcher's shop and buy meat for their husbands' dinners. 'No, it's only for him, that's too good', they would say, rejecting the prime cuts. Birdy never wanted to be dismissed in the same way. But you wonder afterwards: Who was Birdy? What was he really like? Why did he need the protection of such an excuse? Too big a generation gap remains to probe into the answer, as we all consider ourselves kids before him.

* * *

Family histories are a rich source of memories and stories. They can be the easiest way to practise writing outside the demands of writing for work. One of my favourite writers is Stephen Poliakoff whose TV play series *Perfect Strangers* explored the territory inhabited by families, memories and storytelling, and it did this particularly through photography. Unfolding like a detective story, the play shows each of the characters discovering secrets about their families and themselves through black and white photographs from their unknown pasts.

Try this as a writing exercise. Explore those old family albums. In there you will find intriguing images of people you do not know. Perhaps a grandfather, a long-lost cousin, a great-grandma. What are they doing in the photograph? Where are they? Who is with them, in view or out of view? What happened after the photograph was taken? What were they really like? You will find yourself assembling all the necessary elements of a story: characters, plot, location. And who knows where it will take you? Or you can try inventing the story from one of my family photographs, shown here. The photographs also demonstrate the way we live a ritualised existence. Cameras record occasions when families come together for a purpose: whether for births, marriages, seasonal festivals or holidays. These occasions have their own rituals that go back into our collective past.

But there are smaller occasions too that we invest with ritualised meaning. This was particularly brought home to me when I was asked to write a collection of stories for a major food company under the theme 'memorable meals'. The advertising agency DDB wanted me to write these stories not as adverts but to reawaken in their multinational client the emotional importance of food. My brief was to put myself into a number of different fictional personalities to write about the significance of particular meals. Here are three examples:

Joe, 15
I still like to play with food, even if people with me don't recognise the game. I used to eat peas first, then chips, then fish fingers all mashed as a layer across the plate. Nowadays I'm more subtle. Vegetable, meat, potato – in order, but a different order as the plate empties. It's hard to do that and talk at the same time, so I like silent meals. Yesterday I was on my own. Soup stirred three times, each spoonful blown on twice, absolute silence. I loved it.

Peter, 38
Dad came, so we had beef. Mum came, so we had fresh peas.
Josie spent an hour popping the peas into a colander. Aunt Gill
came, so we had broccoli, and Uncle George came so we had
roast potatoes. And we were all there, so we had fruit salad and
ice cream. I still love Sunday dinner. We'd drift apart without it.

Loretta, 42
Bring a dish, I said. It's a good way of bringing people together,
isn't it? The message is a good one too. ... You try my favourite
food, I'll try yours. People arrived with food in casseroles,
pans, storage jars, Tupperware, plates with foil on. There were
samosas next to custard tarts, couscous saying salaam to jerk
chicken, rice cooked in banana leaves opening up to deep-fried
prawns, wontons working the crowd next to Wensleydale with
pineapple.

Everyone joined in. We filled the school hall with a riot of tasty
treats. I sat and listened to the laughter and chatter, I smacked
my lips at the flavours, I breathed in the aromas, I held food in
my fingers that I didn't know by name. But at the end of the
evening we all felt we knew each other just that little bit better.
And we enjoyed each other's food all the more for it.

The stories are fictional. But what is fiction? I know I drew
on memories of my own life even if the characters involved are
not exactly me. Never be afraid to use your own personality and
experience: put them into your writing.

* * *

MONDAY 17TH MAY

A meeting first at the Royal Society of Arts to talk about
their 'day of inspiration' to be held at the Royal Albert Hall in
October. They want me to write the programme and marketing
materials, and to cast an eye over all the words they produce.

Howard Schultz of Starbucks is one of the speakers, and they see me as a link between Starbucks and the RSA, building on the successful Coffee House Challenge programme. The aim of that was to initiate debates in coffee houses nationwide about the RSA's manifesto – promoting the value of informed, intelligent talk to bring about change. Because the RSA had been founded in a London coffee house in 1754, here was an appropriate way to celebrate the RSA's 250th anniversary.

Then in the afternoon a meeting with Kath of Lever Fabergé about storytelling. Apparently the Lever Fabergé directors have redefined their vision and strategy to achieve growth, and a central principle is the role of storytelling to engage people internally and externally with the strategy. I was asked by Kath to give a lunchtime talk and workshop about stories, using examples from my business experience. Fortunately there are now lots of these including the Guinness essence story, the book of which was delivered today.

* * *

A sense of history is a useful skill for a writer to have. Organisations like the RSA obviously have a sense of history, and they have 250 years of it behind them. But a company like Innocent Drinks, five years old, has a history too. The only trick is to use the past to illuminate the present, to be relevant to people today.

It always fascinates me to find out more about the writing habits of writers I admire. The best way to do this is to visit their houses. This brings you closer to them by visiting the actual places where they wrote great books. Dove Cottage in the Lake District, for example, where Wordsworth lived and where Dorothy Wordsworth wrote her daily diary. Like this from exactly 204 years ago to the day that I am writing now.

Sauntered a good deal in the garden, bound carpets, mended old clothes. Read Timon of Athens. *Dried linen. Molly weeded the turnips, John stuck the peas. We had not much sunshine or*

wind, but no rain till seven o'clock, when we had a light shower
just after I set out upon my walk. I did not return but walked
up into the Black Quarter [Easedale]. I sauntered a long time
among the rocks above the church. ... I strolled on, gathered
mosses etc. The quietness and still seclusion of the valley affected
me even to producing the deepest melancholy. I forced myself
from it.

You feel a strong connection with Dorothy Wordsworth
across the centuries, imagining her writing her diary as one
way to force herself out of melancholy. Visit Dickens' houses
in London or Rochester and you sense his personality. Drive
down the Californian coastal highway, drop into Monterey and
imagine a chat with Steinbeck on Cannery Row. Or even, as I
did, run writing workshops for employees of the Bank of Ireland
at the James Joyce Centre in Dublin. Although very few of the
participants had read much Joyce, there was still a sense of awe
in the room.

This communion need not be so historical: modern writers
have interesting things to write about their writing habits. I am
convinced that the sense of ritual, the granting of a special place
to the business of writing, is an important element of being a
writer. Take this example from the novelist Justin Cartwright.

At this moment I am sitting at my desk which is a slightly
worm-eaten French table, with piles of books and bills and
circulars colonising the available table surface, so that only my
computer still rests in a little pool of walnut, jostled on all sides.
I could tidy up, but my mind is on what I am writing – this
article – and it must not be given any opportunity to wander.
As someone once said, preparing to write is not writing, talking
about writing is not writing; only writing is writing. On two
sides overlooking my efforts, are my books. These are the ones
I need for reassurance and for professional purposes – reference
books, favourite books . . .

Very close are my dictionaries in many languages including The Historical Dictionary of American Slang, *volume 1, which covers A to G. I have been meaning for eight years to buy volume 2. If there are any students of my work, they will find that I do not know any American slang which begins with the letters H to Z.*

It's a good joke, of course, although I wager that Justin Cartwright knows 'schnozzle' even without his dictionary's second volume. There is such a traffic, mainly one way, between the USA and the rest of the world. Some people get very agitated about slang and other forms of language that are not absolutely conformist. My attitude, as with foreign words entering English, is laissez-faire. There's no way of stopping slang, and why would anyone want to try anyway? It's simply a case of using language that is appropriate to the context and to the audiences you are writing for. In recent years text messaging has introduced another form of English, and a vibrant one, as long as the sender and the receiver understand the same language. This text poem is by Hetty Hughes and it won the Orange text poem competition.

txtin iz messin
mi headn'me englis,
try2rite essays,
they all come out txtis.
gran not plsed w/letters shes getn,
swears I wrote better
b4 comin2uni
&she's African

Whatever the medium you're using, think about your words. Think who they're written for. Ask yourself questions about them.

Texting makes an important point for me, simply because it comes through a phone. I see all writing as, in a sense, conversation. It's a conversation that you have with a reader.

But, as in a real conversation, there's no cast-iron guarantee that your reader will be reading the message from the conversation that you intend. Margaret Atwood wrote this:

> *Works of literature are recreated by each generation of readers, who make them new by finding fresh messages in them. The act of reading a text is like playing music and listening to it at the same time, and the reader becomes his own interpreter.*

So the readers interpret what you write from their own perspective. Now there's no point complaining about this. The better approach is to recognise it and build your awareness of it into your writing. So always be aware of the possibility of a reader putting a different interpretation onto your words. As you write, conduct a conversation in your head with this reader. This is a strange variant on the idea of hearing voices. It's the writer's Joan of Arc defence – and it is a defence in the sense that it allows you to be more aware of other reactions, so it helps the editing process, which I've emphasised is vital.

* * *

TUESDAY 18TH MAY

Today is the appointed day for judging the 'Writing for design' awards as part of the annual D & AD (Design & Art Direction), the most highly coveted awards in the creative world. The Yellow Pencils that are given (very selectively) in many different categories are much sought after. There's a balance to be struck between maintaining high standards ('Is it good enough for a Yellow Pencil or simply very good?') and not being curmudgeonly (Michael Hockney, the Chief Executive, reminds us of the virtue of generosity).

Having been a jury member twice before for this relatively new (five years old) category, I have now been appointed Foreman of the jury. My role, not precisely specified, is to ensure that winners – in the sense of inclusion in the big annual book and the Yellow Pencil winners (if any) – are up the very highest standards, and to make sure that all the other six members of the jury feel that they have had their say and been listened to.

After many hours of reading and debating, two pieces of work rise above the rest. Labels from Innocent Drinks (of course), maintaining their usual quirkiness. And a report on Corporate Social Responsibility from Westpac Bank in New Zealand. I warmed towards the bank report because the writers had an extremely difficult subject but did not shy away from difficult questions. Indeed those questions – 'What do you want from a bank?' – formed the structure for the 70-page book. The bank told a story. The tone of voice was honest and human. When we are surrounded by puffery on one side and cynicism on the other, the bank's trust in the power of its thinking was impressive.

* * *

Judging other people's work is a humbling responsibility. I've often been on the receiving end of judgements, and no one ever gets all the recognition that they would wish for. Sensitivity to the doubts, fears and expectations of other writers is essential for anyone placed in a position of judgement. This probably means that the best judges are those who don't really want to be judges. But in workshops too, people are understandably sensitive to the judgements of others. That's why it's vital to establish an atmosphere in workshops that enables people to share their work without fear of embarrassment. Writers can help other writers improve by being supportive and constructive. Judge others as you would like to be judged yourself. This does not mean accepting bad writing. It means always striving to make your writing as good as it can possibly be. Learn from other writers. If I were to make an award for 'business writer of the twentieth century', I would give it to David Ogilvy. Here he describes (in 1955) his writing habits to an executive from another advertising agency:

Dear Mr Calt:

On March 22nd you wrote to me asking for some notes on my work habits as a copywriter. They are appalling, as you are about to see:

1. *I have never written an advertisement in the office. Too many interruptions. I do all my writing at home.*
2. *I spend a long time studying the precedents. I look at every advertisement which has appeared for competing products during the past 20 years.*
3. *I am helpless without research material – and the more 'motivational' the better.*
4. *I write out a definition of the problem and a statement of the purpose which I wish the campaign to achieve. Then I go no further until that statement and its principles have been accepted by the client.*
5. *Before actually writing the copy, I write down every conceivable fact and selling idea. Then I get them organised and relate them to research and the copy platform.*
6. *Then I write the headline. As a matter of fact I try to write 20 alternative headlines for every advertisement. And I never select the final headline without asking the opinions of other people in the agency. In some cases I seek the help of the research department and get them to do a split-run on a battery of headlines.*
7. *At this point I can no longer postpone doing the actual copy. So I go home and sit down at my desk. I find myself entirely without ideas. I get bad-tempered. If my wife comes into the room I growl at her. (This has gotten worse since I gave up smoking.)*
8. *I am terrified of producing a lousy advertisement. This causes me to throw away the first 20 attempts.*
9. *If all else fails, I drink half a bottle of rum and play a Handel oratorio on the gramophone. This generally produces an uncontrollable gush of copy.*
10. *Next morning I get up early and edit the gush.*

11. *Then I take the train to New York and my secretary types a draft. (I cannot type, which is very inconvenient.)*
12. *I am a lousy copywriter, but I am a good editor. So I go to work editing my own draft. After four or five editings, it looks good enough to show to the client. If the client changes the copy, I get angry – because I took a lot of trouble writing it, and what I wrote I wrote on purpose.*

Altogether it is a slow and laborious business. I understand that some copywriters have much greater facility.
Yours sincerely
D. O.

* * *

WEDNESDAY 19 MAY

The only day this week when I'm free of meetings and able to do nothing but write. But of course you never actually do nothing but write. Today, with the liberation of time available for writing, I find myself unable to concentrate on any of the work that needs to be done.

So I take a morning break, a coffee at the local Starbucks, a 'rewarding everyday moment'. While there I read the *Daily Mail* and am amazed yet again how the paper's pre-set agenda can pervert good news into bad. 'Big blow for London bid' the banner headline proclaims on the day that London has been included on the shortlist of five for the 2012 Olympics. Intention shapes the words that are used. The paper's purpose – let's undermine the government – gives direction to every word.

Drawing up priorities is difficult, but I write a list of all the smaller tasks that need to be done, the emails to be sent, the people to be telephoned. Then I spend a morning doing those things, clearing the list so that in the afternoon I can focus on the most pressing big project.

In the next month I have a succession of workshops to run for London Underground, the London Development Agency,

Bird's Eye and the BBC. These are on tone of voice, briefing and audience research, but at the heart of them is the idea of storytelling. I eventually got into the right frame of mind to work out the outline of a script and some exercises that with adaptations would work across the different projects.

* * *

Briefs and briefing are vital components of the business writer's everyday life. Briefs vary from simple to complex, short to long, those given over a chat with a cup of coffee to those hammered home by a 60-slide PowerPoint presentation. Most of the briefs I remember fondly simply emerged from a conversation. But for bigger companies especially, the written brief is an essential element of the marketing process.

When thinking about Birds Eye Wall's I wondered if storytelling might be used as part of the briefing process – not only to respond to a brief but to give a brief. I took one of the oldest stories in the world, Homer's *Odyssey*, and broke the story into five parts as seen from the viewpoint of Odysseus:

Problem *'I need to find my way home through unknown seas.'*
Doubt *'I'm weary, I'm lost, I'm scared.'*
Exploration *'I just have to sail and keep sailing, having many adventures, as I look for my home island.'*
Resolution *'Eventually, I find my wife and home, by displaying great courage.'*
Celebration *'Then I'm happy again.'*

Most stories could be described with this five-part structure. I then wondered whether the structure could be applied to a creative brief. Could questions about the expectations for each stage in the story help to create a response to the brief that produced better storytelling?

1. *What is the one unmistakable outcome you want in response to this brief?*
   E.g. We want advertising that makes people think differently about frozen food.
   This gives us a headline statement that sets out the issue, the problem to be addressed.

2. *What are the main questions that arise from probing that headline?*
   E.g. Why do you need to do this? How will people feel differently?
   This clarifies what are the issues in doubt that need to be thought about as a challenge.

3. *Who are the people we're really trying to influence and what are the obstacles to overcome?*
   E.g. We need to focus on the way consumers behave and the demands made on them by today's lifestyle.
   There is a need for thorough exploration to get us closer to the answers.

4. *What answers are we really wanting to find?*
   E.g. We need to set out clearly what our objectives are.
   This will enable us to recognise the resolution when we find it.

5. *What will be the result of a successful resolution?*
   E.g. We want to measure our success in figures and also in terms of how we'll feel.
   This will mean that we can celebrate the outcome.

At the very least, by giving yourself the discipline of allowing only a single sentence answer to each question, you can provide a summary that sets out clearly the expectations of the brief in the form of a story.

Birds Eye wants to change the way people think about frozen food. People don't realise that Birds Eye frozen food is natural food of the highest quality. We'll find ways of changing people's minds so that it becomes a desirable choice. In doing so, we'll make Birds Eye the brand that consumers seek for natural quality and enjoyment. And our consumers will feel warmth and loyalty towards us.

* * *

THURSDAY 20 MAY

An amazing morning at the British Library where we gathered to find out more about a poster project for the London Design Festival. This came about when Lynne Dobney of the LDF asked me if 26, the not-for-profit association of writers for business I co-founded a year ago, would like to collaborate with the ISTD (International Society of Typographical Designers). I was keen to do this, so were 26 and the ISTD, and I suggested that we should produce 26 posters on the individual letters of the alphabet by forming 26 writer/designer teams. Then the British Library offered to host the exhibition of the posters as part of the London Design Festival in September.

The meeting this morning was to introduce the participants to the resources of the Library and to start the creative process. Michelle Brown, curator of manuscripts, gave a wonderful talk about illuminated manuscripts that oozed with her own enthusiasm and knowledge. This was knowledge deeply embedded but lightly worn. Inspiring for all of us. The only problem is that the vastness of the resources available – literally 'the world's knowledge' – is daunting.

In talking about illuminated letters Michelle came up with several thoughts that resonated. In the first millennium, both Islam and Christianity were finding ways to portray divinity without attempting pictorial (but sacrilegious) representations of God. So they celebrated the divine through words. 'They had no problem deciphering a Calvin Klein ad: these people thought in symbols and words to be seen.' Later developments brought in 'historiated initials' where pictures were painted inside a letter to tell a story. Certain letters – B, D, O – had shapes that encouraged this.

I met Gilmar Wendt the designer I have been paired with and we arranged to meet next week to discuss ideas. All the pairings are random and few of the pairs know each other; an appropriate serendipity that might be mirrored by the research process. This afternoon, thinking about ideas, I started to write, my thoughts inspired by the fact that my letter 'N' seems to be the most negative letter of the alphabet. How can we turn a negative into a positive? It can all be done by mirrors or letters reversing NO to make ON.

* * *

I love the poster project, particularly the idea of 26 writers exploring their pleasure in words by starting with an individual letter.

When I started thinking about N, the word negative kept recurring. Not just the word but the concept. No, non, nada, never, nowhere, niet, niente, nul, nil, nihil. In any language, at least any European language, N negates everything. 'Nothing will come of nothing,' as King Lear says.

But if it is nil by mouth I am not so silent by name, my middle initial is N for Neil. There is a positive aspect to N. It also stands next to O in the alphabet, becoming NO in consequence, but seen in a negative image this turns round to ON. There is a bright inside to N's dark outer appearance.

So I started writing a poem, to explore this positive side of the negative. The title came last. Perhaps 'o no n' should be seen as the last word rather than the first?

The poem is about the positive, life-affirming qualities of N. Without it we are lost. The first three verses of the poem are full of words containing N, expressing N's ability to bring the abstract to life. What happens if we deprive ourselves of N, or if we are forbidden its use? 'There is a positive lack of life.' We need opposites to appreciate other possibilities. We need the negative to enjoy the positive. Remove any letter – N or any of the 26 – and we impoverish life, the alphabet and thought.

I discovered too that N derives from ancient Semitic labourers copying an Egyptian hieroglyph of a snake. Later the Phoenicians developed the alphabet further, representing M as 'water'. Because M and N were linked by their nasal sound they thought of the letters as a pair and the word for 'fish' replaced the snake. So letters are literally living things, to be respected and cherished. Just as the extinction of any one creature – narwhal, snowy owl or nettle butterfly – diminishes nature's totality, we should cherish the whole of life, from A to Z, or we lose our humanity.

N

o no n

N came in one night
blown on the wind
through the window
probably sometime soon
after I was born.

With no n
we can neither scorn
nor score points.
We lose the chance
to entrance or entertain.

N is an ingredient
in everyone's living room
morning, noon and night.

Without n
life is so empty
there is a positive
lack of life.

onon

This was a good start for N. Something completely different might emerge over the next two months. By the time the exhibition of 26 posters appears in the British Library in September, perhaps these origins will be unrecognisable. But already it has reinforced for me the need to care not just for individual words as the building blocks of sentences, but for individual letters as the building blocks of words. I understand better why Georges Perec might have wanted to experiment with his novel that did not use the letter 'e'.

Simply as an exercise, try rewriting a paragraph that you have written today – but deny yourself the use of a favourite letter as you rewrite it. What does this do to your language?

The importance of the individual and the potential of the smallest detail were reinforced for me by another new exhibit I saw at the British Library. The title gives you the flavour: *Add. 17469 A Little Dust Whispered*. The project is by Rachel Liechtenstein, the first Pearson Creative Research Fellow at the British Library. Mainly using manuscripts from the Library's collection, she has taken photographs to explore details, acquiring materials such as the imprint of a finger on a page, spores of mould or 'sections of text that had rubbed away, like old stone steps in a church'.

As writers we need to understand that the most vivid connections can be made by the smallest sensory details. Patrick Suskind's novel *Perfume* is a tour-de-force of writing about the sense of smell and its extraordinary embodiment in the character of Grenouille the murderer. All the senses connect to our memories and our imaginations. We all have our individual equivalents of Proust's madeleine cake. When you write, concentrate on details that will evoke pictures in your reader's mind, that will engage with your reader's senses.

Care for detail. It's different from pedantry. If you start worrying about the choice between two similar words, you are showing the inclinations of a writer. When Donna Tartt was interviewed about her novel *The Little Friend*, she said the following:

> *The deepest satisfaction I get out of writing is in the smallest, humblest, most intimate levels – getting a tricky sentence exactly right. I can move a comma around very happily for hours.*

Can you see commas as your friends? Can you love language so much that you want to play with it? Do you want your words to speak for you more effectively than they have done before? Well, you can, if you believe you can.

* * *

FRIDAY 21 MAY

Another day for D & AD judging, this time for Gold Awards – the best of the winners from all the different categories representing the variety of disciplines in advertising and design. In the big room at Billingsgate, typography rubs shoulders with TV commercials, press ads with corporate identity, writing for design with photography. Looking around, the sight of all the work selected is baffling; there is too much to take in. Yet this selection is the absolute tip of the iceberg. Thousands of people will be cursing the various judges because their work hasn't made it this far.

It seemed that there was no obvious candidate for a Gold Award, not at least from the design juries. Perhaps the advertising juries would produce the gold. After all, I had seen there my favourite piece of work, a press ad for Honda with elegant words written on a banana about the power of dreams. I would be happy for this to be well awarded.

* * *

I write by hand, using a pencil. Other people can write only on a keyboard. I love paper. The Honda advert shows the joy of discovering other materials to write on, and this has been an obsession since humans started to depict their lives on the walls of caves. There are certainly no right or wrong materials, but it's worth experimenting to see what suits you best and to carry on experimenting. Try writing on a banana.

It will be clear by now that I am not leading towards a set of rules. Many of the angels rebelled against that, they lost their bright innocence, but gained the ability to experiment with new possibilities, and made our status as dark angels inevitable. I will not be bringing tablets of stone down from the mountain, carrying commandments of what to do or not to do. All my advice is simply advice. The best I can do is describe what has worked for me, and what has worked for other writers. But *you* will find what works best for you.

I have kept my diary in this chapter for one week, Friday to Friday. In between I have referred to writers and books that I find inspiring. If you want to become a better writer at work nothing is more important than reading more outside work. Read great books. That's as close to a rule as I will get. Read the reviews to see what new books are out, then read the books that sound interesting in those reviews. Read those classic novels that you might have shied away from at school – try them now and you'll probably find that books like *Great Expectations*, *Le Grand Meaulnes* and *The Great Gatsby* really do live up to the adjective in their titles.

I can think of no better way to end this chapter than to invite you to read my favourite ending to a book. Soak in the achingly beautiful luxury of the final page of F. Scott Fitzgerald's *The Great Gatsby*.

And as I sat there brooding on the old, unknown world, I thought of Gatsby's wonder when he first picked out the green light at the end of Daisy's dock. He had come a long way to this blue lawn, and his dream must have seemed so close that he could hardly fail to grasp it. He did not know that it was already behind him, somewhere back in that vast obscurity beyond the city, where the dark fields of the republic rolled on under the night.

Gatsby believed in the green light, the orgastic future that year by year recedes before us. It eluded us then, but that's no matter – tomorrow we will run faster, stretch out our arms further ... And one fine morning –

So we beat on, boats against the current, borne back ceaselessly into the past.

Chapter 7
Earning your wings

The other day I was heading down into the Underground station on the escalator. Just across the way a little boy was travelling up the other escalator, holding his father's hand. I caught only the first part of what the boy was saying before the escalators carried him out of earshot. 'Dad, when I grow up will I be allowed to …' I'll never find out what he was going to have to wait to do.

We continue feeling like that little boy for a lot of the time, taking our fears and doubts into adulthood. The greatest problem I encounter with people on writing workshops is a refusal to accept that their companies and their managers will allow them to experiment more with their writing. To use a phrase that is close to jargon, they cannot accept that they 'have permission' to be adventurous. Persuading people that they really do have that permission can be difficult: they really want to believe me but they know their company and its culture. Perhaps because I come from a background in brand consultancy, I insist that the brand values have to be treated as having real meaning, not simply a cosmetic purpose. And, if brand managers and owners are challenged on this, they will agree that indeed they do give permission for more expressive writing to reflect their brand. To choose some values that seem to recur regularly, how can a brand be 'inspiring', 'risk-taking', 'creative', 'personal' if it does not allow the brand's representatives to use language that will give reality to those values? For the whole idea of branding to maintain its credibility, much more support and encouragement needs to be given to the people who write on behalf of brands – and encouragement to take risks with language in doing so.

Otherwise we do become exactly like that little boy on the escalator, yearning to be allowed to try something out but accepting that his lot is to be refused permission. Sometimes it is simply a matter of daring to try something different even if you feel the unwritten company rule book will be used against you. The important thing is to dare to produce writing that is as good as you want it to be – not as mediocre as you imagine the company allows it to be. You should always have permission to strive for high standards in writing for business. The comments in *The Observer* by Mark Haddon (author of *The Curious Incident of the Dog in the Night-time*) are relevant to this argument:

> *The best question I ever received came from a boy who asked whether I did much crossing out. I explained that most of my work consisted of crossing out and that crossing out was the secret of all good writing.*

Of course, we grow up. We grow into adult things like jobs and contracts. Because adults like to keep matters under control. 'No, you can't do that. Wait till you grow up to be a chief executive.' We haven't yet recognised it, but we have effectively what are two kinds of working contract these days.

The first contract is a legal document that says you will be employed until the contract is terminated. That contract is necessary (on both sides) but it still represents something of a threat – a threat that, if you don't do things right, the company will end the contract and dismiss you.

The other kind of contract is rarely written down. It is more of a promise than a threat, a promise that the company that employs you will do as much as it can to help your personal development. With this contract the benefits can be perceived to be more on the employees' side of the court. They can take advantage of personal development opportunities, positioning themselves to leap into completely different careers, even within the same company.

In reality, though, the benefits are much more mutual. The company and the employee realise that they need each other, so they collaborate to each other's advantage. The staff member who keeps developing, not just by acquiring skills closely related to the day job but by gaining a broader vision and becoming more open to fresh ideas, is not only a more satisfied employee but almost certainly more effective on the company's behalf.

I hope this is actually the true meaning that lies behind

'human resources'. The term has been with us some time now without ever gaining complete acceptance. There is something uncomfortable in a term that seems to define people so clearly as a resource.

John Humphrys, the scourge of politicians in radio interviews, recently tore into the subject:

> *It is an outrage that the phrase 'human resources' was not strangled at birth. I hate it for its ugliness and its sloppiness. A moment's thought tells you that 'resources' are exploited, used up, squeezed for every last drop of value and then replaced. Are we really meant to regard human beings in that light? It seems we are.*

That tirade comes from the introduction to *Between You and I: A Little Book of Bad English* by James Cochrane. Where John Humphrys gets it wrong, I believe, is that he misunderstands the word 'resources' – or at least he does not allow it enough potential for meaning. There is an irony there in that he is berating the world for sloppy use of English but neglecting to see that 'resources' is a much richer word than he implies through his narrow interpretation. That's a problem with 'Plain English' – it can be too plain.

For one thing, the environmental debate, which he glances towards, is about ways in which we can avoid exhaustion of the planet and move towards more renewable or sustainable resources. Just as with the planet, we need to have a respectful, compassionate approach to human resources – or companies will find them disappearing.

The other latent meaning in 'resources' is simply an ability to draw on one's own resources – resourcefulness, if you like. The *Oxford English Dictionary* defines that meaning of resources as: *capability in adapting means to ends, or in meeting difficulties.*

It seems to me that a capability to adapt means to ends and to meet difficulties is a quality most companies should cherish in their people. In return, help in achieving that is what most people also yearn for from their companies. This shift towards

realising mutual development was well-established by John
Scully of Apple:

> *The new corporate contract is that we'll offer you an opportunity
> to express yourself and grow, if you promise to leash yourself to
> our dream, at least for a while.*

We express our dreams through images and words, primarily
through words. Writers are better than most at expressing
dreams. Through writing we try to recreate the vividness of a
dream although dreams can never be pinned down. But you can
get closer to expressing them vividly, in ways that make better
sense to you and to others around you – and that increases
your self-esteem and the esteem in which you are held by
colleagues.

Writing has extraordinary potential, if we can just find the
right ways to release its creative power in people, particularly
in people who might not consider themselves to be creative
writers.

In a strange way it becomes easier to understand the
transforming potential of writing at work by looking at
examples of people who are deprived of a workplace. Mark
Salzman recently described, in *True Notebooks,* his work as a
creative writer working with the young inmates of a Los Angeles
penitentiary. This is an inspiring story of writing's ability to give
people a voice even when locked away in a place that denies
them liberty, independent judgement and hope. For these are
not petty criminals, they are mainly young people who have
been punished for taking the lives of other human beings. Yet
they can express feelings like this in a writing class:

> *There are many reasons why I write. Some are unexplainable,
> others I can explain are my way of expressing emotion, my way
> of getting free, my mental vacation, my way to vent anger, my
> way to throw emotional blows without using my physical ability,
> a way that no one gets hurt. A way to get through life and keep
> the peace. It's my joy, my shining light. If I had no pencil and*

paper my mind would fail, with no real vocals to express myself
it would overload my brain. My writing is how I maintain.

That was written by a prisoner called Carlos Bours. The
writing is raw, not particularly elegant, but it becomes tempting
to start using words like 'redemption'. Yet I want to keep my
case for writing in the context of the workplace. The argument
for greater creativity through writing at work is a compelling
one that does not need the reinforcement, or possibly the
distraction, of a more general social benefit.

It comes down to a belief in humanity. By suppressing
creative expression at work, or at least failing to give it
sufficient encouragement, managers and companies are limiting
the human potential of their employees. The reality is that
employees' expectations have risen. Although the job for life
went some time ago, people now expect their job to add to
the quality of their life. This means that they want to pursue
more of their individual interests at work, putting their own
personalities into the contracted hours.

The changing structure of employment reinforces this. More
and more of us work in the 'service' industries, which means we
are in the business of providing service. So employers look for
real service skills, understanding and empathy, skills that come
from inside rather than being imposed. And this means giving
people the encouragement and permission to bring more of
their humanity into their working life.

This automatically implies enabling people to be more
creative. Our creativity – our ability to think, generate ideas
and express them – is what distinguishes us as human beings.
The 'human resources' we seek are surely creative resources
because we are not after automatons at work. All organisations
want thinking, expressive individuals able to provide ideas
and solutions. This applies just as much to, say, a lawyer as an
advertising executive, a sales assistant as a designer.

The surest way to unlock this creativity is through writing.
We all have to write at work. We can all benefit ourselves and
our organisations if we become more creative in our business

writing. We need to recognise writing not just as a competency to develop but as a means to liberate people at work to express more of their innate creativity.

Of course, this raises other issues that might be uncomfortable to face in corporate life. It forces us to try to understand and come to terms with the nature of our humanity – and with the knowledge that our individuality can be an unpredictable, not easily manageable force. In any management system currently known to the business world, that requires extraordinary confidence and self-belief to encourage. It demands great managing editors as well as great writers at work.

Yet our humanity is the reality that we live with. Can we be content with a management system that allows more human expression to some than to others? After all, human beings consider themselves unique individuals, and it is the creative impulse that defines our uniqueness. There is arrogance implicit in this, of course, that returns me to my theme and that confirms our status as dark angels. For whereas an angel gives unquestioning obedience to a higher power, even the most self-effacing of human beings have deep-seated beliefs in their own uniqueness. 'I' is such an important word and concept that we often hide it inside the pronoun 'we'.

For me dark angels are human beings; human beings are dark angels. We are not heavenly angels because we are neither 'good' enough nor obedient enough to be so. Nor are we fallen angels, we are not inherently 'evil' in that way, and the powers we have are by definition human not superhuman. Yet we have been touched by both kinds of angel, we understand both possibilities, we are blessed and cursed with knowledge and experience.

My starting point was Milton's *Paradise Lost* and Philip Pullman's storytelling in reaction to some of the religious orthodoxy in Milton's poem. Both are magnificent creative works, human and darkly angelic in their soaring ambition. But we should remember the historical context for *Paradise Lost*. John Milton was a Puritan Christian who did not believe in the divine right of kings. As a regicide, his endorsement of the execution of King Charles I put him firmly in the anti-authority rebel camp – in effect a rebel angel revolting against the force of the established church that saw the king as the embodiment of God on earth. This explains some of the sympathy we feel Milton invested in his portrayal of Satan.

He did not go as far as his poetic admirer William Blake would have gone. *Paradise Lost* is still a justification of God's decision to punish Man for disobedience, whereas Blake would have made the narrative theme one of human regeneration.

In the modern age, we are more comfortable with the idea that humans are flawed but potentially divine – capable of seeking perfection. We have all been made with a spiritual dimension, with enormous imaginative potential and with a moral sense. But we find it hard always to live up to those possibilities.

Milton talks of Satan's angels as Apostate, lost, rebel, fallen and bad. By dark angels I do not mean the Apostate, lost, rebel, fallen and bad followers of Satan. I mean we ordinary human beings who are neither divine nor infernal but have been shown both possibilities. Because we have knowledge we can rise to a higher state; we can at least aspire to the power, invention and subtlety of angels. Perhaps our knowledge is given an added dimension because we have been made dark, less innocent, by our association with the rebel angels. We have a power of questioning and a thirst for discovery that grows from experience, and we use them to develop and express ourselves creatively.

My argument is to accept and be happy with this fate. It gives us the world: the world inside our own heads. Creativity is a gift we need to value and respect in every human being. We all have it; we are all capable of nurturing it further. There are many ways to develop creativity but my belief is that most of us have an activity and a situation that provide us with a relatively easy opportunity. We can express our creativity powerfully, easily and effectively through writing at work. It is there, an activity that we all need to do as part of life. And we could do it particularly during that large part of our life that is spent at work. We could do it so much better, if only we were allowed to.

But we are allowed to. We have that permission. Let us explore our potential through words, words that soar off the page, fly out of the screen, into the imaginations of others. Let us live up to our abilities as dark angels.

PS: Never forget to read

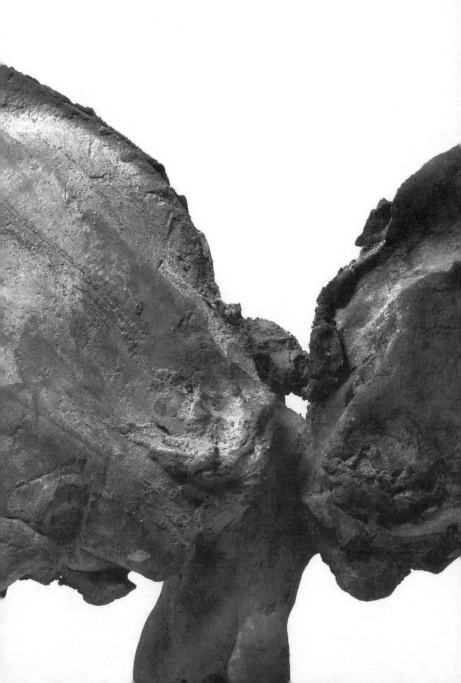

Reading is vital if you want to improve your writing. Two books that were inspirations for *Dark Angels* were *Paradise Lost* by John Milton and *His Dark Materials* by Philip Pullman. In a *Guardian* article, Philip Pullman recently wrote:

> *If human beings can affect the climate, we can certainly affect the language, and those of us who use it professionally are responsible for looking after it.*

Books that I have read while writing *Dark Angels* include:

Oracle Night by Paul Auster

Any Human Heart by William Boyd

Fever Tree by Jackie Wills

By Grand Central Station I Sat Down and Wept by Elizabeth Smart

Middlesex by Jeffrey Eugenides

The World According to Garp by John Irving

Brick Lane by Monica Ali

The Curious Incident of the Dog in the Night-time by Mark Haddon

True Notebooks by Mark Salzman

Kid by Simon Armitage

Tipping the Velvet by Sarah Waters

I enjoyed them all and each must have influenced my writing a little. Thanks to Stuart Delves who shamed me into finally reading James Joyce's *Ulysses*, which I completed over many weeks either side of the Bloomsday centenary on 16 June 2004.

Other kinds of writing are important too. Charlie Kaufman's film scripts are always intriguing on the role of the writer. I enjoyed *Adaptation* and *Eternal Sunshine of the Spotless Mind* a lot. Two plays over this period, both at the National Theatre, were outstanding, making me think, laugh and cry: Martin McDonagh's *The Pillowman* and Alan Bennett's *The History Boys*. See them if you get a chance.

Acknowledgements

I would like to thank the following for the use of extracts reproduced in this book.

Joni Mitchell *Hejira* published by Warner Bros Publications.

Bob Dylan *Positively 4th Street* published by Sony Music Entertainment Inc.

Steve Reich and Beryl Korot *Three Tales* © Copyright by Hendon Music, Inc. a Boosey & Hawkes Company. Reproduced by Boosey & Hawkes Music Publishers Ltd.

Maura Dooley 'What every woman should carry' from *Sound Barrier: Poems 1982–2002* by Maura Dooley (Bloodaxe Books, 2002).

E. E. Cummings *i thank You God for most this amazing* is reprinted from *COMPLETE POEMS 1904 to 1962* by E. E. Cummings, edited by George J. Firmage, by permission of W. W. Norton & Company. Copyright © 1991 by the Trustees for E. E. Cummings Trust and George James Firmage.

Plain English Code by permission of the Plain English Campaign.

Stephen King *On Writing* published by Hodder & Stoughton, 2001.

Jeffrey Eugenides *Middlesex* published by Bloomsbury.

James Flint 'The Accident' published by Zembla Magazine.

Jackie Wills 'Recession' from *Fever Tree* published by Arc Publications.

Maxence Fermine *Snow* published by acorn book company.

Simon Hoggart *Playing to the Gallery* published by Guardian Books. Used by the permission of Grove Atlantic Ltd.

Pieces of Intelligence: The Existential Poetry of Donald H. Rumsfeld, compiled and edited by Hart Seely, published by Simon & Schuster.

Margaret Atwood *Negotiating with the Dead*, 2002, published by Cambridge University Press.

David Ogilvy *The Unpublished David Ogilvy* edited Joel Raphaelson, copyright © 1986 by The Ogilvy Group, Inc. Used by permission of Crown Publishers, a division of Random House, Inc.

F. Scott Fitzgerald *The Great Gatsby* published by Penguin.

John Humphrys from *Between you and I* by James Cochrane published by Icon Books.

Mark Salzman *True Notebooks* published by Bloomsbury.

My thanks too to everyone on the Arvon week in March 2004, especially to the following for permission to reproduce their work: Katherine Mellor, Kevin Benfield, Will Dallimore, Caroline Triptree, Jayne Workman, Laura Forman, Tim Rich and Stuart Delves.

Strenuous efforts have been made to contact all copyright holders and we apologise if any have been inadvertently overlooked.

Index

My Sisters'a Barista
How they made starbucks a home from home

John Simmons

Coffee is a commodity. You can get a cup at any café, sandwich bar or restaurant anywhere. So how did Starbucks manage to reinvent coffee as a whole new experience, and create a hugely successful brand in the process?

My Sister's a Barista tells the Starbucks story from its origins in a Seattle fish market to its growing global presence today. This is a story that has unfolded quickly – at least in terms of conventional business development. Starbucks is a phenomenon. Unknown 15 years ago, it now ranks among the 100 most valuable brands in the world. It has become the quintessential brand of the modern age, built around the creation of an experience that can be consistently reproduced across the world.

In exploring the secrets behind Starbucks' success, this book also tackles the wider question of what makes a successful brand. But ultimately, it is a fascinating human story to inspire all of us.

> *'Sometimes we forget brands have stories to tell and are, in fact, stories themselves. John Simmons brings stories to life in ways that are fresh, bold and inspiring.'*
> [Jon Potter, Global Brand Director, Guinness]

> *'Sit down with a cup of coffee, put your feet up, and be prepared to be riveted by the story of Starbucks. A fascinating read, by a fascinating writer.'*
> [Rita Clifton, Chairman, Interbrand]

UK £7.99

26 Letters
Illuminating the Alphabet

Edited by Freda Sack, John Simmons and Tim Rich

How often do we think about the individual letters of the alphabet? What are their histories, their personalities, their stories? What does C mean to you? Where did X come from? How does N make you feel?

The writing group 26 and the International Society of Typographic Designers have joined forces to explore the DNA of language. Twenty-six business writers have been randomly paired with twenty-six graphic designers, given one letter each and asked to create a collaborative work that celebrated, explored, questioned, elucidated or subverted that letter. In a series of diary pieces, the pairs wrote about the excitement and frustration, the research and the concepts, the relationships and the techniques that led to the finished works.

This book is a celebration of creative partnership based on a neglected aspect of our lives: the twenty-six letters that convey information, express emotion and enable us to function in the world. Amid the variety of contributions, what shines through is a love of letters, their look and their meaning, and the gift of pleasure that they offer to us all.

Throughout the process, the British Library acted as a resource for information and inspiration, and the resulting exhibition, "26 Letters: Illuminating the Alphabet," is being displayed throughout the library building as part of the 2004 London Design Festival.

UK £14.99

Designers

Roger Fawcett-Tang
Christine Fent
Morag Myerscough
David Quay
Lucienne Roberts
Paul Austin & Ben Parker
Nick Bell
Nokia Design, Brand Team
Derek Birdsall
Christian Altmann & Stuart Youngs
Marksteen Adamson
Tom Green
Angus Hyland
Gilmar Wendt
Rick Sellars
Bryan Edmondson
Alan Fletcher
Michael Johnson
Erik Spiekermann
Henrik Kubel
Peter Dawson
Lila Szagun
Alan Kitching
Thomas Manss
Brian Webb
Alan Dye

Writers

Sean Lewis
Mark Fiddes
Charlotte Rawlins
Gordon Kerr
Tom Lynham
Laura Forman
Mark Griffiths
Martin Lee
Jim Davies
Will Awdry
Neil Taylor
Mary Whenman
Sarah McCartney
John Simmons
Tim Rich
Robert Williams
Jamie Jauncey
Roger Horberry
Howard Fletcher
John Spencer
Dan Germain
Stuart Delves
Dan Radley
Mike Reed
Margaret Oscar
Alastair Creamer

Now use your wings